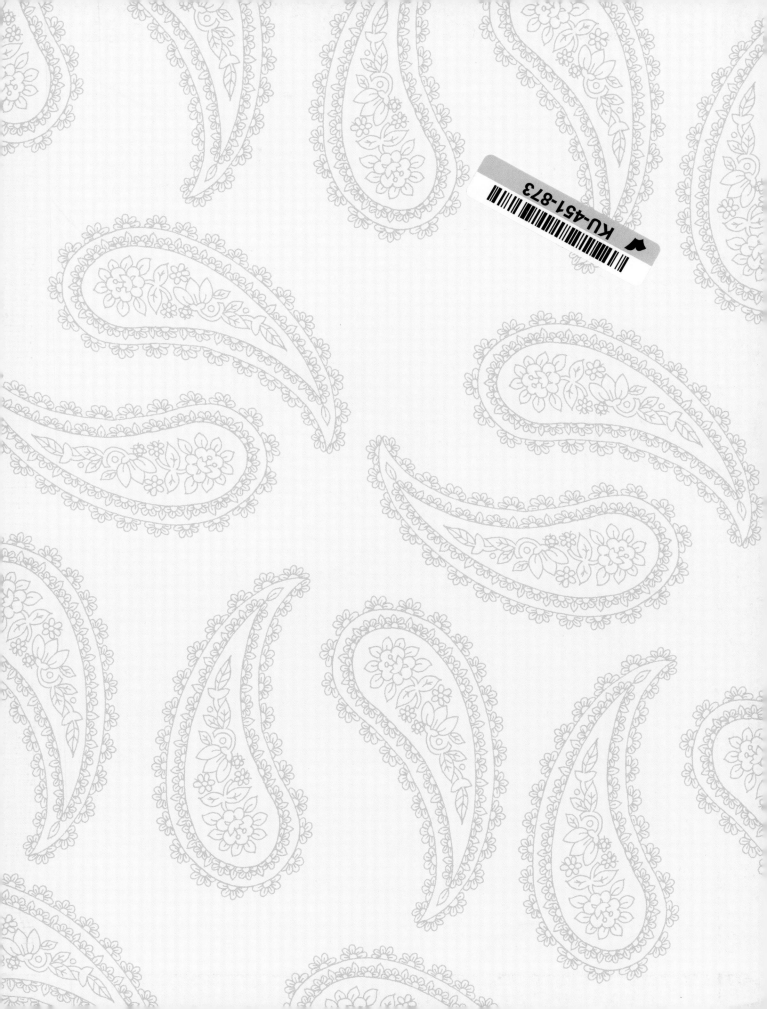

3d Rubber Stamping

Joanne
Sanderson

David and Charles

www.mycraftivity.com

A DAVID & CHARLES BOOK
Copyright © David & Charles Limited 2008

David & Charles is an F+W Publications Inc. company
4700 East Galbraith Road
Cincinnati, OH 45236

First published in the UK in 2008
First published in the US in 2008

Text copyright © Joanne Sanderson, 2008
Photography and layout copyright © David & Charles, 2008

ISBN-13: 978-0-7153-2866-8 hardback
ISBN-10: 0-7153-2866-2 hardback

ISBN-13: 978-0-7153-2864-4 paperback
ISBN-10: 0-7153-2864-6 paperback

Printed in China by SNP Leefung Pte Ltd
for David & Charles
Brunel House, Newton Abbot, Devon

Commissioning Editor: Jane Trollope
Desk Editor: Emily Rae
Assistant Editor: Sarah Wedlake
Project Editor: Ame Verso
Art Editor: Sarah Clark
Designers: Joanna Ley and Emma Sandquest
Indexer: Ingrid Lock
Production Controller: Beverley Richardson

Visit our website at www.davidandcharles.co.uk

David & Charles books are available from all good bookshops; alternatively you can contact our Orderline on 0870 9908222 or write to us at FREEPOST EX2 110, D&C Direct, Newton Abbot, TQ12 4ZZ (no stamp required UK only); US customers call 800-289-0963 and Canadian customers call 800-840-5220.

To my daughter Rianna.
Thank you for your patience
– I love you so much.

Contents

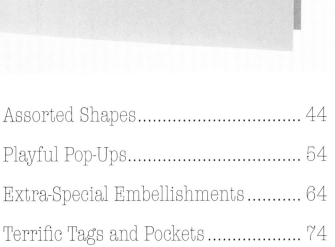

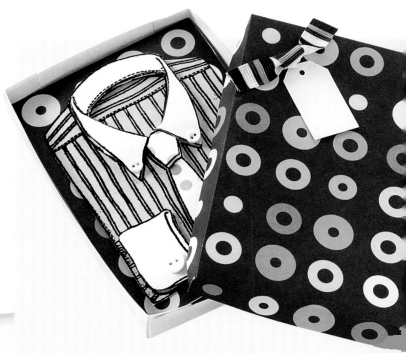

Introduction

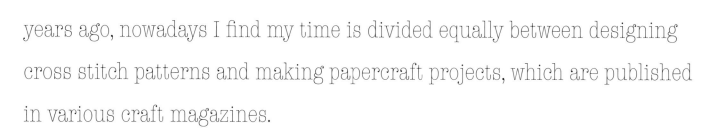

For as long as I can remember I have found immense pleasure in creating things. As a child I would sit and draw for hours, I made my own cards, painted, and explored numerous other craft media. Although I started out as a cross stitch designer nine years ago, nowadays I find my time is divided equally between designing cross stitch patterns and making papercraft projects, which are published in various craft magazines.

Rubber stamping has become one of my favourite ways to express my creativity. I love the versatility of the humble rubber stamp and the fact that stamps are available in such a vast range of styles and themes. Thanks to the variety of inks, images can be produced on a whole multitude of surfaces such as glass, fabric, wood, card and more. One of the charms of rubber stamping is that you don't have to be able to draw to produce beautiful images, and simple colouring techniques can help you create stunning works of art in a very short space of time.

This book is intended for everyone – from those who have never attempted stamping before to more experienced stampers. I hope that the following projects offer inspiration and a starting point for ideas, as well as a chance to explore new techniques. As with all crafts, the aim is to have fun and there is no right or wrong. If I make a mistake I never throw it away but find that I can somehow adapt it to use in a different way, and I hope you will gain the confidence to do this too.

The project chapters that follow are devoted to different aspects of producing three-dimensional stamped cards and gifts, ranging from simple layering techniques to more complex methods of shaping paper to make boxes and pop-ups. Following the projects in chapter order will provide a home workshop, as each chapter combines techniques covered in previous chapters. Alternatively, the more experienced crafter can pick out individual projects to work from and use the ideas as a springboard for their own creations. Techniques are explained in more detail in the Stamping School section and Stamp Smart tips offering further advice and inspiration can be found throughout.

Getting Started

All that you really need to start stamping is some paper or card, a few stamps and an ink pad or two. However, a basic craft tool kit will help you turn your simple stamped images into creative cards and gorgeous gifts. This chapter looks at the equipment you will need to begin stamping with success, as well as the initial techniques required to make the projects in this book. Further techniques, including applying colour and tearing paper, can be found in the Stamping School on pages 112–17.

Rubber stamps

Available in a wide range of themes and styles, rubber stamps usually fall into two categories. Firstly, ones containing outline images, which can then be coloured in, and secondly, solid stamps, which produce a bold, flat image. The images produced by the second type are usually less detailed than the outline stamps, but just as effective. Shadow stamps fall in to the second category and consist of simple images that provide a background for other stamps.

Mounted stamps (right) include traditional wooden stamps. The stamps consist of a rubber die layer containing the image, which sits on a foam cushion. This is mounted on a wooden block; a picture of the image is usually printed on top of the block.

Rubber stamps

Available in a wide range of themes and styles, rubber stamps usually fall into two categories. Firstly, ones containing outline images, which can then be coloured in, and secondly, solid stamps, which produce a bold, flat image. The images produced by the second type are usually less detailed than the outline stamps, but

just as effective. Shadow stamps fall in to the second category and consist of simple images that provide a background for other stamps.

stamp smart

When choosing any type of stamp ensure that the die is deeply etched, as this will produce clean, even images when stamped.

CLEANING STAMPS

With proper care stamps should last a lifetime. They should be cleaned after each use and stored away from direct sunlight and heat. Not only will this prolong the life of the stamp, it will also ensure that ink from previous projects don't muddy the current image. Never soak wooden stamps in water as this may loosen the die; a wipe with a damp paper towel or an alcohol-free baby wipe will suffice. Permanent inks can be removed using specialist stamp cleaners. To avoid the rubber perishing, always make sure the stamp is dry before storing it away.

Inks

Ink comes in an almost endless range of colours – in both single pads and rainbow versions, which contain four or five colours to produce a variegated stamped image. Stamping works on many different surfaces, depending upon the type of ink used. Specialist inks are available that are designed to work with materials such as acetate, leather, shrink plastic, vellum, glossy card, glass, wood, metal and fabric (see Mix & Match Materials, pages 92–103).

Pigment ink pads

Pigment inks are slow drying and work wonderfully with heat embossing, where specialist powder is sprinkled on to the wet ink and melted with a heat gun (see Heat embossing, page 15). The ink is usually rich and produces crisp, vibrant images. This type of ink works best on porous matte paper or card, as it often doesn't dry on glossy or coated surfaces (unless embossing powder is to be used). Metallic inks belong in this group, as do chalk and pearlescent inks.

Speciality inks

Embossing inks can be clear or tinted; they dry slowly and are used with embossing powder, which is then heated to create a raised waterproof image. Embossing ink is available in pad and pen form.

Resist inks repel water-based dye inks on glossy paper. Resist ink such as VersaMark™ produces a soft watermark effect on coloured card or paper. It is slow drying and slightly sticky and so is ideal for projects that are going to be coloured by chalk, the effect being that the VersaMark™ will darken the chalked image while the background will remain subtle (see Chalks, page 114). Paint powders such as Perfect Pearls™ will achieve similar results.

Permanent solvent inks can be applied to most surfaces including vellum, shrink plastic, wood, acetate, metal and glossy card. It is fast-drying ink, making it unsuitable for heat embossing. StazOn® is an example of this type of ink – no heat setting is necessary, and because it is waterproof it is suitable for making images that are going to be painted afterwards. A specialist stamp cleaner should be used to clean the stamps. This type of ink should always be used in a well-ventilated room.

Fabric inks are designed specifically for fabric use, although if making projects that won't require washing some dye inks can be used. It is often necessary to pre-wash the fabric and then set the ink with heat after stamping.

Dye ink pads

These water-based inks dry quite quickly on most types of paper, and are usually permanent and waterproof. They are ideal for stamping an image that is going to be coloured by watercolour paints or pencils afterwards (see Applying colour, pages 113–14). Dye inks are usually acid free and so work well with scrapbook projects, although do check with the manufacturer first. Dye inks soak into porous paper, which achieves a slightly softer result when dry, and because they are fast drying they can often be applied to glossy or coated card surfaces, including vellum. Shadow inks are a type of dye ink that have soft, subtle colour and are designed to work with background or shadow stamps.

Paper

Paper is divided in to three weights: light, medium and heavy. The thickness is measured in microns (mic) and the weight in grams per square metre (gsm). When selecting paper and card for any craft project consider its use – the colour, texture and weight are all-important and will affect the end result. Plain, smooth, medium-weight white card is ideal when a clear, crisp stamped image is required. If the card is fairly thick it will also take paint, whereas thinner cards and papers may buckle – this is also noticeable when heat embossing. Paper and card contain a grain in the same way that fabric does. To find the grain, gently bend the paper lengthways and then widthways – whichever way bends the easiest is the direction of the grain. It is important to know which way the grain lies, as the neatest folds and tears are made when they lie along the grain rather than against it.

Types of paper

Handmade paper tends to be porous and often contains dried leaves and petals, as well as rag or recycled paper. Mulberry paper can produce a lovely feathered edge effect when torn (see Tearing, page 116).

Vellum is a translucent non-porous paper and is commonly used in parchment crafts. It produces a fantastic frosted effect when embossed. When ink is applied to vellum it will be slow drying and so specialist inks are needed when stamping (see Mix & Match Materials, pages 100–101). Avoid using glue on vellum as it will show and can sometimes cause buckling. If it cannot be avoided, hide the glue with ribbon or other embellishments.

Watercolour paper is a heavyweight paper that is designed to be wetted without stretching and is therefore suitable for painting on. It is available in different weights and textures. Very rough textured paper will not give a crisp, even print when stamped, and so images with very fine lines should be stamped on to smooth watercolour paper. Thick cartridge paper will also take a light wash of paint.

Decorative craft papers include stardust papers, felt paper, holographic, shimmer, metallic and pearlescent papers. They are available in different weights and thickness.

Scrapbook paper also varies in thickness and some types are double-sided with different patterns or colours on the reverse, making them ideal for fancy folding techniques, such as origami or iris folding. Scrapbook paper often has a white core when exposed, and so can be used to produce a chamfered-edge effect (see Tearing, page 116). It is possible to stamp on to scrapbook paper; however some coated papers may need to be heat embossed or stamped using solvent inks, which will dry on almost any surface.

MAKING A FOLDED CARD

Many of the projects in this book require you to make a single-fold base card. To do this, cut a piece of card the height of the finished card, but twice the width. Mark the centre line and score using a bone folder or embossing tool and a ruler. Scoring the card first will give a neater fold. Specialist boards often have markings for making complex folds such as gatefold and concertina cards and gift boxes, and while these are not essential they do produce great results in seconds.

Basic craft equipment

There are thousands of different craft tools available, all designed for slightly different purposes. You don't need to spend a huge amount of money on your tools though. In reality, many items can be used for the same purpose, so which tools you want to invest in is really down to personal choice.

Cutting equipment

A craft knife/scalpel (right) is good for making precision cuts, to cut around edges or for cutting small sections from the centre of images.

A self-healing cutting mat (right) protects the work area when using a craft knife. Choose one with a grid marked on it together with a metal ruler (below) to produce a straight edge when cutting. The grid makes it easy to obtain accurate paper sizes and borders when layering.

Craft scissors (right) in a standard size will suit most purposes. Sharp pointed scissors with a straight or curved blade are ideal for découpage. Decorative-edged scissors can add visual interest and there is a wide variety to choose from.

Guillotines and trimmers (below) make it quicker and neater to achieve a straight edge than with a pair of scissors or craft knife. Trimmers are available in a number of sizes; some guillotines also have interchangeable decorative blades to give wavy or perforated edges. Guillotines and trimmers usually have a grid or markings to help with measuring.

Rotary cutters (below left) are used in conjunction with a cutting mat and metal ruler. The handle is similar to a craft knife and the cut is achieved by rolling the wheel along the edge of the ruler on the paper. By changing the wheel the cut can be altered from straight to deckle or even a perforated finish.

Oval and circle cutters (below left) work by placing a cutter inside a template and turning it a complete rotation within the template.

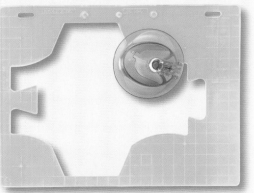

stamp smart

When using scissors a cleaner cut is produced by making one cut using the full length of the blade. With decorative-edged scissors, line the scissors up with the last cut to obtain a neat and continuous edge, making a complete cut along the blade.

Decorative punches (right) cut out shapes from lightweight paper and are available in many forms and sizes. They can also be used to make negative spaces within a paper border. Long reach punches are available, which enable the shape to be cut further from the edge. These are good for cutting apertures into single-fold cards or creating negative confetti-style shapes randomly over the front of a card. Single holed plier punches are used for putting holes in card to make gift tags.

Lightweight die cutting machines (below) are based on a similar principle as decorative punches, however the dies tend to be more elaborate and can cut through a wider range of materials of varying thicknesses in seconds. Some of these machines also take brass embossing stencils.

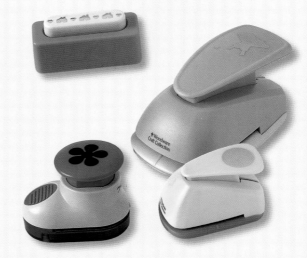

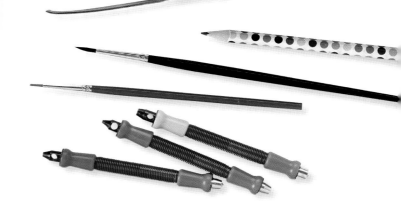

stamp smart

When you need to see exactly where you are punching, turn the punch over. It is then easy to line up the punch with the patterns on the paper. Save the cut outs for use as embellishments in other projects. If the punch becomes blunt, sharpen it by punching through aluminium foil a few times.

General craft tools

Bone folders (right) are flat tools that are used to score creases in paper and card. There are many specialist boards on the market that are used in conjunction with a bone folder to measure creases accurately and to achieve elaborate folds, such as a gatefold.

Tweezers (right) are ideal for placing layered and découpage images, lifting outline stickers, placing gems and beads, and pulling wire or ribbon through punched holes.

Brushes (right) are useful not only for painting stamped images, but also for applying pearlescent powders, brushing away excess embossing powder and stippling colour to produce a background for stamping on to.

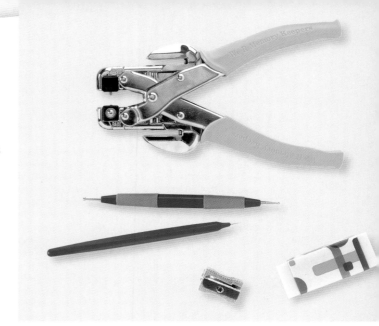

Embossing tools (right) are used in the technique of dry embossing (see Dry embossing, page 117), when used with a stencil. They are also useful for scoring card and for frosting vellum. Embossing tools can also be used for indenting foil (see page 103).

Eyelet fixing tools (right) are used for attaching eyelets to hold layers of card together or purely for decoration. The traditional eyelet fixer consists of a setting tool, which is used in conjunction with a small hammer. One end of the tool has a punch to make a hole and the other end sets the eyelet once it is placed in the hole. Spring-loaded eyelet tools are also available, eliminating the need for the hammer. A range of different-sized tools is available.

Needles and piercing tools (right) can be used for making simple stitches through card or paper, and for applying tiny amounts of glue to embellishments such as beads. Paper piercing tools are also available for pricking holes into paper, which can create a pattern in itself.

PVA glue is water-based glue that dries clear. It can be used to secure objects such as charms and pressed flowers to card and paper, découpage images and collage-style projects. It can be diluted with water to make a clear varnish, but this can stretch the paper so care is needed.

Glitter glue is glitter suspended in clear glue; it is mainly used for colouring items rather than as an adhesive, and tends to be slow drying.

Aerosol adhesives (left) are good for sticking paper images and photographs down and should only be used in well-ventilated spaces. Re-positional as well as permanent varieties are available.

Sticker machines (left) are available in different sizes and have either re-positional or permanent adhesive cartridges. Place many small items together in the tray to reduce adhesive waste. These machines are good for sticking small punched shapes on to card. They eliminate much of the mess associated with glue and there is no drying time.

A pencil, sharpener and eraser (right) are essential for marking measurements. Use a soft pencil that won't scratch the card or paper and is easily erased. Ensure that the pencil has a sharp point for greater accuracy. Keep the eraser as clean as possible to avoid dirty marks and smudges.

Glues and adhesives

Adhesives are available to suit many different purposes and come in acid-free form to protect heritage and scrapbook projects. Always read the label to ensure that the product is suitable.

A glue stick (above) is a quick-drying adhesive used for sticking lightweight paper together. It usually dries clear.

stamp smart
Very thin paper can be strengthened by running it through a sticker machine and then placing it on to thicker backing card or paper.

stamp smart

When using aerosol adhesive it can be difficult to control its application. Place the item you are gluing upside down in an old shoe box before spraying to prevent the work area and the materials on it from being coated in glue.

Embellishments and decorative fixings

Embellishments will really enhance your 3D projects. A wide variety of purpose-made trimmings are available from craft stores, including beads, gems, ribbons, wire, threads, pegs, shells and leaves.

Buttons and charms (left) can be used to secure mini envelopes and work well in collage-style projects. They are fixed with a stitch, a blob of glue, a glue dot, or can be suspended from wire or thread.

Brads (below) are decorative fasteners that are inserted into a hole in the paper and secured by bending the wings out on the reverse.

Eyelets (below) are ring-shaped fasteners. They all work on the same principle – first a hole is made, the eyelet ring is dropped into the hole and then secured by flattening it with an eyelet setter.

Other stamping tools

Brush markers are a good way of colouring solid stamps and allow more control than ink pads when placing colour on the stamp (see Using brush markers, page 15).

Embossing powders (page 14) are used to heat emboss stamped images where slow-drying ink has been used, such as pigment or embossing ink (see Heat embossing, page 15). Avoid using embossing powder with dye inks as they are too fast drying to achieve a good result. It is important to remember not to overheat the powder, as a dull rather than shiny image will be the result. Heating time will depend on your heat gun and the powder used. Once the powder melts, immediately move the gun away to another area. Embossing powders are available in a range of colours, from clear through to metallic and sparkle effects.

Glue dots are available on a roll and come in different sizes. There are non-permanent, and permanent varieties as well as acid-free dots. Press the embellishment on to the dot, peel the dot from the backing roll and secure to the card or paper.

Double-sided tape is often used to stick mats or mounts together, as it is less messy than glue and doesn't require drying time. Sheets of double-sided tape are also available on to which glitter or micro beads can be shaken to create sparkly self-sticking paper. Metal leaf can also be applied to these sheets to produce an exquisite effect (see page 98).

3D foam pads give a raised effect to a project and are often used in découpage and layering. They are sticky on both sides and work in the same way as double-sided tape but are thicker. These types of pads are often difficult to remove if a mistake is made, so care is needed.

A heat gun (right) is used to melt embossing powder. Overuse can scorch the paper or card and so care needs to be taken. Keep the gun moving slowly over the surface to avoid this, and remember protect the work surface underneath. Heat guns are also used to 'set' slow-drying ink and to activate shrink plastic (see page 96).

A stamp positioner, although not essential, is a handy tool that enables precise positioning of stamps when creating a repeat motif pattern or border.

A brayer (right) is a useful tool for applying an even coat of ink to larger stamps (see Brayering, page 113).

A mist bottle is useful for spraying water on to a stamp after inking. The resulting image has a slightly unpredictable, soft watercolour effect.

How to stamp

The basic techniques of inking stamps and heat embossing images are all you really need to get started on the projects in this book. Once you have your stamped and embossed images, advice on applying colour is given in the Stamping School on pages 113–15.

Using an ink pad
The primary technique of stamping from an ink pad is crucial to master if you want to produce crisp images.

1 Hold the stamp face up and with the other hand gently tap the stamp with the ink pad. Check that the whole surface is evenly covered with ink. Remove any ink from the edges of the stamp (caused by over inking) with a paper towel.

2 Apply the stamp to the paper in one movement using firm even pressure, without rocking or sliding the stamp.

3 Carefully lift the stamp from the paper to reveal the image.

Using brush markers

Colouring the stamp with brush markers allows more control over where the colour is placed on the stamp. Numerous different colours can be added before stamping.

1 Apply colour on to the stamp with the brush markers.

2 Breathe a 'huff' on to the stamp to remoisten the ink (or spritz it gently with a mist bottle) prior to stamping.

3 Press the stamp firmly on to the paper to produce the image.

Heat embossing

This method produces raised patterns on paper and card. The image is either drawn by hand using an embossing pen or a stamp is inked using slow-drying pigment ink or embossing ink before being sprinkled with embossing powder. The powder is then melted with a heat gun. If the powder used is semi-transparent or clear then the underlying ink will be seen.

1 Stamp the image on to card using a pigment or embossing ink.

2 Sprinkle embossing powder over the image and gently tap or shake off the excess on to a piece of paper. Return the unused powder to its container.

3 Place the stamped image on a protected surface and holding the heat gun a few inches away, carefully move the gun around the image until the powder melts.

4 Once the powder has melted and cooled, the image can be coloured using the chosen medium (see Applying colour, pages 113–15).

Resist embossing

This technique uses clear embossing ink and powder to preserve the colour of the background card, which is then coloured.

1 Ink the stamp with clear embossing ink. Sprinkle clear embossing powder over the image and gently tap or shake off the excess, returning the unused powder to its container. Heat with a heat gun until the powder melts.

2 When the image has cooled, apply ink using a sponge or pad directly on to the paper. A brayer can be used to apply the ink (see Brayering, page 113).

3 Use absorbent kitchen paper to rub the image – the excess ink is removed to reveal an embossed image that is the same colour as the original card.

stamp smart
Try the resist embossing technique using coloured card and contrasting ink. Using glossy paper and rainbow dye ink pads to colour the paper produces fabulous results.

TIPS FOR EXCELLENT EMBOSSING

- Before stamping, use an anti-static cloth to wipe the card – this will reduce the risk of embossing powder sticking to other parts of the card.
- A heat gun is essential for heat embossing. Do not try to use a hairdryer, as this will simply blow the powder away.
- Do not overheat the powder or the image will appear dull and you may scorch the paper. Heat until the powder melts, then stop.

Lavish Layering

Probably the simplest way of adding depth to any project is by placing layers of card or paper on top of each other. Each layer should be progressively smaller than the layer below it, producing borders of alternating colour: dark colours on top of light and vice versa. For dramatic results use a limited palette and vary the depth of the border with each layer. It is usually desirable for the borders to be equal on all four sides – when layering up different elements getting the spacing right between the pieces will create balance.

Bags of Love

Layers of white, silver and pink card form the basis of this project. A little handbag adds three-dimensional interest and is made simply by folding a single piece of card that has been cut using a die cutting machine. Alternatively, a ready-made shop-bought item could be used. By using different shaped punches you could change the theme from hearts to butterflies, dragonflies or even balloons.

1 Use the pink ink pad to carefully ink the paisley stamp, ensuring that the rubber is evenly coated. Stamp the image on to one of the square pieces of white card.

2 Trace the template on pag 118 on to translucent tracing paper. Using a soft pencil, rub the reverse side of the image (the back of the paper) over the area where the shape is drawn. Place the tracing paper on to the stamped card face up. Use a pencil or embossing tool to re-draw the heart carefully following the outine on the paper. When the paper is removed the shape will have been transferred on to the stamped card. Cut around the outline carefully.

YOU WILL NEED

Elusive Images 'UA4GW0157(c)' stamp sheet • Rose pink ink pad • Three pieces of white card, one 13 x 26cm (5⅛ x 10¼in) for the base card, and two 10.5cm (4⅛in) square • Silver card 11.5cm (4½in) square • Mid-pink card 12cm (4¾in) square • White stripe embossed card 15 x 14cm (5⅞ x 5½in) • Small strips of card 2cm (¾in) wide, one each in pale pink, mid-pink and silver • Sizzix™ Big Shot Thick Cuts 'Purse' die and die cutting machine • Woodware small and medium heart punches • Spool of thin silver wire • Cocktail stick • Double-sided tape or glue stick • 3D foam pads

FINISHED SIZE 13cm (5⅛in) square

3 Layer the stamped heart centrally on to the second square piece of white card. Layer again on to the square of silver card and then on to the square of mid-pink card. Secure each layer with a glue stick or double-sided tape.

4 Score then fold the large rectangular piece of white card in half to make the base card. For a crisper edge use a bone folder.

5 Use the Purse die to cut and assemble a handbag from the white stripe embossed card. Using double-sided tape on the tabs instead of glue will ensure that the tabs will stick instantly without having to hold them while waiting for the glue to dry. Cut a 2cm (¾in) square from the strip of pale pink card and glue to the front of the handbag.

6 Using the small heart punch create three pale pink, two mid-pink and one silver heart from the strips of card.

7 Wrap the silver wire around the cocktail stick to make a spring. Trim the wire at the desired length and carefully remove it from the stick. Repeat until five springs of differing lengths have been made.

8 Secure the springs on to the inside of the handbag using double-sided tape. Glue the handbag centrally on to the large stamped heart and use 3D foam pads to stick the small pink hearts to the springs. Punch a medium heart from the stamped offcuts and glue to the front of the handbag and secure the small silver heart on top.

FROM THE HEART

A charming gift tag, ideal for a wedding, anniversary, engagement or Valentine occasion, can be made using the same techniques. A large heart punch is used to create the central heart and the springs are made in exactly the same way as the main card. A piece of ribbon threaded through a punched hole will allow you to secure it to your gift for a truly personal touch.

stamp smart

Experiment with bolder colour schemes and different patterned stamps to create diverse results, but remember to use similar coloured ink to the card used if you want a harmonious effect. Silver card and wire gives a contemporary feel, whereas gold or copper would give a more antique look.

Funky Fashion

The colour scheme of this clothes-themed card is simple and girly. The image is stamped directly on to fabric-patterned scrapbook paper and 3D foam pads are used to secure the layers, creating a sense of depth. The garments are secured with tiny pieces of foam so that they can move, almost like real fabric.

1 Use the VersaMark™ ink pad to stamp the images on to the smaller pieces of scrapbook paper.

2 Use the black embossing powder to heat emboss the images, one at a time.

3 Carefully trim around the edges of the stamped images as close to the outline as possible. Shape the wire into a simple coat hanger shape and secure it behind the blouse using double-sided tape.

4 Fold the large piece of white card in half to make the base card. Cut the heart from the RMSCB376 paper and layer on to the RMSCB226 paper, layer on to the remaining piece of white card and attach the brads in opposite corners. Layer on to the Flavia paper and then on to the blue sparkle paper using the 3D foam pads. Stick centrally on to the front of the base card using double-sided tape.

5 Use the 3D foam pads to stick the clothes on to the front and apply the gemstones.

stamp smart

When trimming around the outline of a heat-embossed image take care not to chip the melted powder.

....

YOU WILL NEED

Elusive Images 'UAGHC0002' stamp sheet and clear acrylic mounting block • VersaMark™ ink pad • Black embossing powder • Sandylion scrapbook papers 'RMSCB376' and 'RMSCB313' 10 x 5cm (4 x 2in), 'RMSCB226' 8 x 5.5cm (3⅛ x 2⅛in), and 'RMSCB227' 7 x 5cm (2¾ x 2in) • Colorbök® 'Flavia Peaches and Pomegranates' paper 11 x 8.5cm (4⅜ x 3⅜in) • Blue sparkle paper 11.5 x 9.5cm (4½ x 3¾in) • Two pieces of white card, one 13 x 21cm (5⅛ x 8¼in) for the base card, and one 8.5 x 6cm (3⅜ x 2⅜in) • Silver-coloured wire 10cm (4in) in length • Two pink brads • Four clear adhesive gemstones • Double-sided tape or glue stick • 3D foam pads

FINISHED SIZE 13 x 10.5cm (5⅛ x 4⅛in)

....

Best Friends

This fun stamp and jigsaw die are the perfect combination for a unique card. The stamped image is gently coloured and layered on to pretty scrapbook paper. Use different images and papers to create themed cards for other occasions.

stamp smart

For an alternative idea, the pieces of the jigsaw can be left unassembled and placed in an envelope, which is then stuck on to the front of the base card. Decorate the envelope with the same stamped image.

1 Use the black ink pad to stamp the image on to the smaller piece of white card.

2 Colour the image with the pencils and apply a little water with a brush to blend. Glue on to the stiff card.

3 Using the jigsaw die, cut the layered image to make the jigsaw pieces.

4 Fold the larger piece of white card in half to make the base card. Cover the front with the larger piece of scrapbook paper. Glue the smaller piece at an angle on top. Glue the turquoise card on to the front of the card at a slightly different angle to the scrapbook paper and glue the jigsaw pieces directly on to it. Leave the jigsaw incomplete by sticking one of the pieces at a slight angle away from the rest.

5 Make a small bow from the ribbon and glue on to the front of the card to finish.

YOU WILL NEED

Penny Black '2887K' stamp • StazOn® black ink pad • Two pieces of white card, one 21 x 15cm (8¼ x 5⅞in) for the base card, and one 8 x 11.5cm (3⅛ x 4½in) • Two pieces of The English Paper Company 'All Occasion' scrapbook paper, one 10.5 x 15cm (4⅛ x 5⅞in), and one 8 x 11.5cm (3⅛ x 4½in) • Turquoise card 8 x 11.5cm (3⅛ x 4½in) • Stiff card 8 x 11.5cm (3⅛ x 4½in) • Sizzix™ jigsaw die and die cutting machine • Watercolour pencils in pink, grey, blue, green and yellow • Narrow lilac ribbon 15cm (5⅞in) in length • Glue stick

FINISHED SIZE 10.5 x 15cm (4⅛ x 5⅞in)

Cool Music

When used with VersaMark™ ink, clear embossing powder produces a lovely resist effect, preserving the colour of the background paper when paints are applied over the top. This pretty collage-style stamp is cut and layered repeatedly using 3D foam pads to enhance the three-dimensional quality of the card.

YOU WILL NEED

Penny Black '2390L Music Collage' stamp • Penny Black '2025M Music Background' stamp • Inca Stamps '566-AA Treble Clef' • VersaMark™ ink pad • Funstamps Verdi Gris embossing powder • Clear embossing powder • Five pieces of white card, one 14 x 17cm (5½ x 6⅝in) for the base card, and four 15 x 7cm (5⅞ x 2¾in), plus a small scrap • Watercolour paints in yellow and blue • 3D foam pads

FINISHED SIZE 14 x 8.5cm (5½ x 3⅜in)

1 Fold the large piece of white card in half to make the base card. Use the VersaMark™ ink pad to stamp the Music Background image on to the front of the base card.

2 Use the Verdi Gris embossing powder to heat emboss the image.

3 Using the VersaMark™ ink pad, stamp the Music Collage image on to three pieces of white card. Use the clear embossing powder to heat emboss the images. Stamp the image again on to the remaining piece of white card but this time use the Verdi Gris embossing powder to heat emboss the image.

4 Use the brush to dampen each piece of card with water. Using a watery mixture, apply the paints to each image allowing the colours to mingle together softly.

5 Once the images are dry, cut out each layer making them progressively smaller so that different parts of the image are revealed on each layer. Use 3D foam pads to stick the layers together, carefully aligning each layer with the image underneath.

6 Finally, use the VersaMark™ ink pad and Verdi Gris embossing powder to stamp and heat emboss the Treble Clef on to a small scrap of white card. Secure on to the front of the card with 3D foam pads to finish.

BOLD SQUARES

This bookmark is made from leftover scraps of paper from the main card. The pieces are torn then glued on to black card, allowing parts of the card to show in between the pieces. They are then cut into squares and layered on to coloured card. Graphic images are stamped and heat embossed using gold embossing powder. *Stamps used: Whispers 'Swirl' and Woodware 'Daisy Block'.*

The Cat's Whiskers

The layered effect of this card is achieved simply by folding over the top corner of the base card. By covering the inside with a different coloured paper to the front you can exaggerate the result. Use bright, cheerful colours with distinct patterns to achieve the maximum impact.

1 Use the black ink pad to stamp the image on to the small square of white card. Colour the image with the pencils and apply a little water with a brush to blend. Cut out around the edge of the image.

2 Layer the image on to the orange square and then on to the blue square of paper.

3 Fold the large piece of white card in half to make the base card. Cover the inside right-hand side of the card with the orange paper and the inside left-hand side with the spotted paper. Cover the front of the base card with the striped paper.

4 Using the top right-hand corner as the starting point, measure 7cm (2¾in) along the top and down the side of the card, join the points to make a diagonal line and fold over the edge on to the front of the card.

5 Secure the layered stamped image on to the folded flap with glue or double-sided tape. Take care not to apply tape or glue to the top or right-hand side of the image so that it doesn't stick to the inside of the card when it is closed flat.

6 Glue or tape the strip of the spotted paper on to the front of the card and finish by securing the button on to the left-hand side of the strip.

YOU WILL NEED

Hero Arts® 'LL078 Cat Portrait' stamp • StazOn® black ink pad • Six pieces of Making Memories® 'Kids Max' paper, three pieces (one orange, one striped and one spotted) 15 x 10.5cm (5⅞ x 4⅛in), one strip 1.5cm x 10.5cm (½ x 4⅛in) (spotted), one 5cm (2in) square (orange), and one 5.5cm (2⅛in) square (blue) • Two pieces of white card, one 15 x 21cm (5⅞ x 8¼in) for the base card, and one 5cm (2in) square • Making Memories® blue/green ribbon and ribbon brads pack • Watercolour pencils in orange, yellow, blue and green • Double-sided tape or glue stick

FINISHED SIZE 15 x 10.5cm (5⅞ x 4⅛in)

stamp smart
Painting the image with similar colours found in the patterned paper will help to unify the design.

Graphic Hearts

Coloured ink and bold graphic stamps are used to make this quick and simple heart-themed card. Suitable for any romantic occasion from a loved one's birthday to a Valentine, it would also make a modern and stylish wedding or engagement party invitation card.

YOU WILL NEED

Hero Arts® 'LL187 Fancy Hearts' stamps • Hero Arts® 'LL041 Graphic Blocks Borders' stamp • Brilliance 'Pearlescent Orchid' pigment ink pad • ColorBox® 'Cranberry' pigment ink pad • Mid-pink card 14 x 21cm (5½ x 8¼in) for the base card • Four pieces of white card, three 5.5 x 4cm (2⅛ x 1½in), and one 3.5 x 10.5cm (1⅜ x 4⅛in) • Dark pink card 4.5 x 10.5cm (1¾ x 4⅛in) • Colorbök® 'Flavia Peaches and Pomegranates' paper 7 x 10.5cm (2¾ x 4⅛in) • 3D foam pads • Glue stick

FINISHED SIZE 14 x 10.5cm (5½ x 4⅛in)

stamp smart

The hearts could be stamped and heat embossed using coloured or metallic inks and powders to achieve a slightly different look. Change the colour scheme to white and silver for a contemporary wedding or anniversary card.

1 Use the Cranberry ink pad to stamp each of the images on to the three small pieces of white card. Trim around the outline of each heart.

2 Using the Pearlescent Orchid ink pad, stamp the Graphic Block Border on to the strip of white card. Layer on to the dark pink card to make the border.

3 Fold the mid-pink card in half to make the base card. Glue the Flavia paper 1cm (⅜in) down from the top of the front of the card.

4 Using the 3D foam pads, stick the hearts on to the border and then stick the border centrally on to the Flavia paper on the front of the base card.

TWO HEARTS COLLIDE

A matching gift tag or place setting card can be made using the same materials. The Flavia paper is used as the base card and is decorated using the stamped hearts and a ribbon bow. 3D foam pads are used to layer the hearts on top of one another.

Wonderful Weave

Strips of decorated paper are woven together to make a pretty background for this card, which is a clever way of using up leftover scraps from other stamping projects. The central focal point is made from a punched flower and gold brad. This card uses a similar technique to the bookmark shown on page 22, but instead of cutting the paper into squares it is cut as strips and woven together.

stamp smart

Add interest by varying the tones of the scraps and adding a touch of metallic embossing powder and card to the layers.

YOU WILL NEED

Whispers 'Spiral' stamp • Woodware 'Daisy Block' stamp • Hero Arts® 'LL927 Conversation Dots' stamp • VersaMark™ ink pad • Gold embossing powder • Three pieces of white card, one 13 x 26cm (5⅛ x 10¼in) for the base card, and two 13cm (5⅛in) square • Deep pink paper 13cm (5⅛in) square, plus a small scrap • Two pieces of gold card, one 12.5cm (5in) square and one 6cm (2⅜in) square • Large flower punch • Gold brad • Scraps of stamped images leftover from other projects • Glue stick

FINISHED SIZE 13cm (5⅛in) square

1 Use a glue stick to adhere torn pieces of stamped scraps leftover from other projects on to one of the squares of white card. Allow for gaps in between the pieces so that the white paper shows through. Allow the glue to dry and then cut into 2.5cm (1in) strips.

2 Cut the deep pink paper into 2.5cm (1in) strips. Lay the strips vertically on to the square of white card and then place the white strips horizontally, weaving each piece under and then over each pink strip. Glue the whole thing down carefully on to the other square of white card and trim the edges to neaten.

3 Using the VersaMark™ ink pad and gold embossing powder, stamp and heat emboss the images randomly over the woven strips.

4 Fold the large piece of white card in half to make the base card. Layer the woven strips on to the gold card and then on to the front of the base card.

5 Glue the small gold square on to the front of the base card. Cut a 3.5cm (1⅜in) square from one of the stamped off-cuts and use 3D foam pads to stick it in the centre of the gold square.

6 Punch a flower from the scrap of deep pink paper, secure the brad in the centre and stick on to the base card using a 3D foam pad.

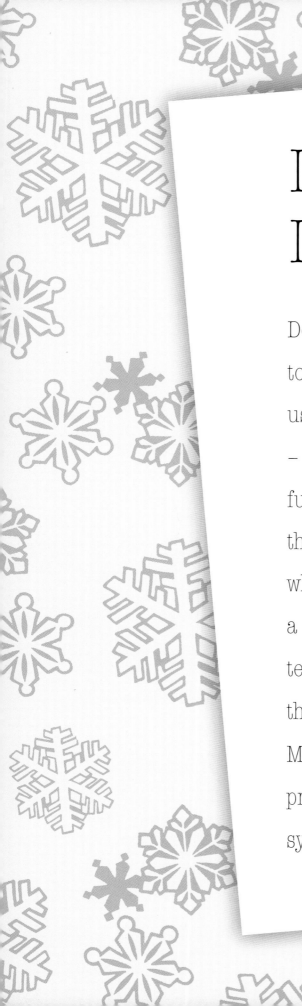

Dimensional Découpage

Découpage – derived from the French *découper*, to cut out – is the art of cutting out images and using them to decorate any items that you wish – from cards and boxes, to candles and even furniture. Three-dimensional découpage involves the layering of multiple copies of the same image, which get progressively smaller to produce a raised effect. When choosing images for this technique, the ones with definite outlines are the easiest to use, as they are simpler to cut out. Medallion stamps are perfect for découpage-style projects because of their solid outlines and symmetrical patterns.

Festive Medallion

Here, a medallion stamp is combined with glitter and simple layering of each cut-out image to create an attractive Christmas tree decoration. Using dark red and green gives a traditional look, but a more contemporary colour scheme of icy blues and lilacs with silver embossing powder would work equally well.

stamp smart

The more layers the ornament has the more three-dimensional and bauble-like it will appear. To complete your bauble, add a tassel at the bottom by sandwiching it between the two decorations before sticking them together.

YOU WILL NEED

Elusive Images 'JCW0003' stamp • VersaMark™ ink pad • Gold embossing powder • Two sheets of pale green card A4 size (29.7 x 21cm / 11⅝ x 8¼in) • Two sheets of white card A4 size (29.7 x 21cm / 11⅝ x 8¼in) • Red and green fine glitter • Art Glitter Adhesive and fine-tip applicator • Dark red ribbon or cord 20cm (8in) in length • 3D foam pads • Double-sided tape or glue stick

FINISHED SIZE 8cm (3⅛in) diameter

1 Use the VersaMark™ ink pad to carefully ink the stamp, ensuring that the rubber is evenly coated. Stamp the image on to the pale green card.

2 Sprinkle gold embossing powder over the stamped image and tap off the excess powder, returning it to the container. Remove any stray powder with a paint brush. Heat with the heat gun until the powder melts. Repeat this process alternating between green and white card until you have at least six embossed images.

3 Cut out each layer, so that each image is progressively smaller. Depending on where the image is cut, different effects can be achieved.

4 Use the fine-tip applicator to fill in the outer edges of the largest image stamped on to the green card with Art Glitter Adhesive. Sprinkle the green glitter on to the wet glue, tap off the excess returning it to the container. Leave to one side and allow to dry completely. Repeat this with each green layer. Use the red glitter to embellish the white layers in exactly the same way.

5 Once the layers are completely dry, starting with the largest green image at the bottom, layer the second largest white image on top using 3D foam pads. Repeat with each image in alternate colours until the last and smallest image is in place.

6 Repeat steps 1–5 to make a second complete layered image. Attach the cord or ribbon on to the back of one of the decorations using glue or double-sided tape. Attach the completed decorations back to back so that the ribbon is sandwiched between them. The ornament is now ready for hanging.

TIPS FOR MARVELLOUS MEDALLIONS

- Medallion stamps can be coloured in a number of different ways, just as other stamps (see Applying colour, page 113–15). To save time, only add colour to the areas that will be seen and not to areas that will be hidden by the layers above.
- Take extra care when cutting out stamped and heat-embossed medallions. Trim as close to the outline as possible without chipping the embossing powder.
- Bold contrasting card used in alternate layers will give a more dramatic effect with these stamps and works well when areas of pale glitter are added.

Water Lily Wishes

A medallion stamp is layered again in this project, but this time to make a contemporary card. To add further appeal, smaller complementary images are stamped directly on to the front of the base card and then heat embossed.

1 Use the VersaMark™ ink pad to stamp the image on to one of the square pieces of white card.

2 Use the gold embossing powder to heat emboss the image. Repeat this process until you have an embossed image on all three squares of white card.

3 Cut out each layer so that each image is progressively smaller. Depending on where the image is cut, different effects can be achieved.

4 Use the fine-tip applicator to fill in the outer edges of the largest image with Art Glitter Adhesive. Sprinkle the darkest red glitter on to the wet glue, tap off the excess returning it to the container. Repeat this process on each image, filling different areas with varying shades of the glitter. Leave to one side to dry.

5 When completely dry, layer the images together using 3D foam pads, starting with the largest image at the bottom, until the smallest image is at the top.

6 Fold the large piece of white card in half to make the base card. Stick the layered image on to the front, slightly off centre, using 3D foam pads.

7 Using the same ink and embossing powder, stamp and heat emboss three smaller images from the sheet on to scraps of white card and apply the glitter in the same way. Once dry, cut around the edges of the images and then stick them randomly on to the front of the card using 3D foam pads.

8 Using one of the other small stamps from the sheet, stamp and heat emboss the image directly on to the front of the card randomly in between the other images, with some disappearing off the edge of the card.

YOU WILL NEED

Elusive Images 'Waterlily Mandala' stamp sheet and clear acrylic mounting block • VersaMark™ ink pad • Gold embossing powder • Four pieces of white card, one 13 x 26cm (5⅛ x 10¼in) for the base card, and three 12cm (4¾in) square, plus scraps • Art Institute Glitter Kit in Monochromatic Red • Art Glitter Adhesive and fine-tip applicator • 3D foam pads

FINISHED SIZE 13cm (5⅛in) square

Twisting Carnations

The image from this stamp is made up into a box, and parts of the image are layered again for a great 3D effect. The box shown here has four sides but the image could be stamped five or even six times to produce a pentagonal or hexagonal box.

1 Use the VersaMark™ ink pad to stamp the image on to the cream card.

2 Use the green embossing powder to heat emboss the image. Repeat the process until there are five stamped and heat-embossed images. Trim around the edge of each image close to the outline.

3 Using the H20 paints carefully paint the design. Once dry, take four of the images, fold the side flaps over and glue each piece together. Working clockwise, place each of the bottom flaps on top of the previous one and tuck the final flap under the first to secure.

4 Cut out the flowers from the fifth image, layer on to the front side of the box aligning carefully over the first image and secure them with 3D foam pads. Use glitter glue to highlight areas of the pattern and then allow to dry.

5 Wrap the ribbon around the box and tie to make a bow. Make a small tag shape from the deep pink card (see page 78), pierce or punch a small hole in the top, thread the beads and narrow ribbon through the top and tie to secure. Add the rosebuds and a message to the tag and then glue on to the top of the box to finish.

YOU WILL NEED

Creative Expressions 'HH1176L' stamp • VersaMark™ ink pad • Green embossing powder • Two sheets of cream medium-weight card A4 size (29.7 x 21cm / 11⅝ x 8¼in) • Deep pink card 4 x 2cm (1½ x ¾in) • Twinkling H20 paints in 'Sea Green' and 'Cherry Sorbet' • Glitter glue • Pink ribbon 50cm (20in) in length • Two small paper rosebuds • Narrow pink ribbon 10cm (4in) in length • String of plastic pearl beads 10cm (4in) in length • 3D foam pads • Glue stick

FINISHED SIZE 9.5 x 6 x 6cm (3¾ x 2⅜ x 2⅜in)

Butterfly Posy

Butterflies are great to use as 3D découpage images, particularly over an aperture where the wings look almost as if they are flying. Using watercolour paints complements the soft effect of the background paper. Painting is much easier when embossing powder is used, as the paint stays within the outline.

1 Use the VersaMark™ ink pad to stamp the image on to the white smooth card.

2 Use the black embossing powder to heat emboss the image. Repeat the process until there are three images on the card. Trim around the edge of each image close to the outline. Paint each layer with the paints and allow to dry.

3 Leave the first image intact. Cut the small leaf and grass stem from the second image. On the third image remove the top set of wings and antennae from the butterfly and the two background leaves and grass stem. Use 3D foam pads to stick each layer together, starting with the complete layer at the bottom and ending with the smallest layer at the top.

4 Cut out the embossed centre panel from the front of the base card. Glue the scrapbook paper on to the inside right-hand side of the base card so that it will show through the aperture.

5 Carefully glue the left-hand wing of the butterfly on to the front of the card ensuring that the other wing and leaves lie partly over the aperture.

stamp smart

A plain white card can be dry embossed using a brass stencil and light box to produce much the same results as this shop-bought base card. Many die cutting machines also take embossing plates, which create a raised outline in seconds.

YOU WILL NEED

Oyster Stamps 'UM1025' and clear acrylic mounting block • VersaMark™ ink pad • Black embossing powder • White smooth card 13cm (5⅛in) square • DCWV 'Dragon Flower' single-fold base card • Paper Adventures 'Pardon My Posies' scrapbook paper 14cm (5½in) square • Watercolour paints in red, orange, yellow and green • 3D foam pads • Glue stick

FINISHED SIZE 14cm (5½in) square

Vase of Flowers

The 3D découpage effect here is achieved by carefully cutting flowers from a second image and gluing them over the first with dots of silicone adhesive, applied with a cocktail stick for greater precision. This simple technique can be applied to almost any stamp.

YOU WILL NEED

Inkadinkado Stamps 'Classic Botanicals' and clear acrylic mounting block • StazOn® black ink pad • Two pieces of white card 10 x 5.5cm (4 x 2⅛in) • Paper Adventures 'Morning in the Garden' paper 11.5 x 7cm (4½ x 2¾in), and 'Bluesy Shadow Wash' card 15 x 21cm (5⅞ x 8¼in) for the base card • Silicone adhesive • Paints or pencils in green, blue, orange, yellow and pink • Glue stick

FINISHED SIZE 15 x 10.5cm (5⅞ x 4⅛in)

stamp smart

Use a very sharp pair of scissors or craft knife to carefully cut out the small flowers. The silicone glue enables the flowers to be placed at very slightly different angles to achieve a more natural effect.

1 Use the black ink pad to stamp the image on to both pieces of white card. Colour both images with the paints or pencils.

2 Cut flowers from the second image and use the silicone adhesive to stick them on to the first image.

3 Fold the Bluesy Shadow Wash card in half to make the base card. Layer the image on to the Morning in the Garden paper and then glue on to the base card to finish.

DECOUPAGE DRAGONFLIES

This frame is made using silver card and silver embossing powder. The aperture is cut away, and the roses and dragonflies are used as embellishments. A second piece of card is cut to make the back and glued on the bottom and side edges only so that a photo can be placed inside. A simple strut is made by gluing a strip of stiff card on to the back. A crease is made 1.5cm (½in) from the top of the strut so that the frame stands. *Stamp used: Stamps Happen Inc 'Dragonfly and Rose'.*

Lovely Leaf

This sophisticated card uses only one stamp and ink pad and is very quick and easy to make. Stamping on scrapbook paper gives a lovely coloured effect without the need for painting the image. When it is layered up, the pattern becomes unpredictable, so that no two cards will be the same.

YOU WILL NEED

Magenta 'M.0469' stamp • StazOn® black ink pad • Magenta 'Spring Rose' paper, three pieces 8cm (3⅛in) square • Dark pink card 14 x 22cm (5½ x 8⅝in) for the base card • Burgundy card 8cm (3⅛in) square • Green card 8.5cm (3⅜in) square • Silicone adhesive • Glue stick

FINISHED SIZE 14 x 11cm (5½ x 4⅜in)

1 Use the black ink pad to stamp the image on to all three pieces of the Spring Rose paper.

2 Leave the first image intact. Trim the leaf, border and ladybird from the second image. On the third image trim the bottom part of the border and part of the leaf. Use silicone adhesive to apply the layers on top of the complete image.

3 Glue the layered image on to the burgundy card. Layer again on to the green card.

4 Fold the piece of dark pink card in half to make the base card and stick the layered image on to the front.

stamp smart

Bend the leaf slightly to enhance its shape before the adhesive is applied. To do this, place it face down in the palm of your hand and gently rub the back in a circular motion using an embossing tool.

ON SAFARI

This gorgeous giraffe image is stamped twice on to patterned paper. The smaller giraffe is then cut out from the second image and layered on to the first with silicone adhesive. The animal-print tiles are also stamped on to the same paper. Thinner papers such as these are best glued to a contrasting card to stiffen them, so that they stay rigid when sticking them down with 3D foam pads. Embossed paper subtly enhances the 3D quality of the card and a simple colour scheme prevents the design looking too busy.
Stamps used: Stamping Sensations 'INR-026'.

Hearts and Flowers

This pretty card uses apertures and découpage stamped images teamed with deep pink and cream papers to produce a stylish result. Stamp sets are great for mixing and matching images and creating lots of different variations. By changing the papers and the placement of the apertures the combinations are almost endless.

YOU WILL NEED

Magenta 'Retro Romance' stamp sheet and clear acrylic mounting block • StazOn® 'Timber Brown' ink pad • VersaMark™ ink pad • Clear embossing powder • Sandylion scrapbook paper – three pieces of 'RMKSCB99', one 5.5cm (2⅛in) square, one 8 x 3cm (3⅛ x 1⅛in), and one 2cm (¾in) square, 'RMKSCB95' 8 x 3cm (3⅛ x 1⅛in), and three pieces of 'RMKSCB96', one 3 x 5cm (1⅛ x 2in), one 8 x 3cm (3⅛ x 1⅛in), and one 5.5cm (2⅛in) square • White card 15 x 21cm (5⅞ x 8¼in) for the base card • Sandylion stickers 'PKGEM15' • Medium and large square punches (optional) • Silicone adhesive • 3D foam pads

FINISHED SIZE 15 x 10.5cm (5⅞ x 4⅛in)

1 Use the brown ink pad to stamp the rose and vase images on to the rectangle of RMKSCB99 paper and trim around the edges. Repeat with the same sized pieces of RMKSCB95 and RMKSCB96 papers. Trim around the vase and rose and layer on to the cream image using silicone adhesive. Repeat for the square heart stamp using the larger square of RMKSCB99 paper and square of RMKSCB96 paper.

2 Use the VersaMark™ ink pad to stamp the script-style image on to the small rectangle of RMKSCB96 paper. Use the clear embossing powder to heat emboss the image. Trim around the edge.

3 Use the brown ink pad to stamp the patterned heart on to the small square of RMKSCB99 paper and trim around the edge following the outline as close as possible.

4 Fold the white card in half to make the base card. Using a sharp craft knife and ruler or punches, cut a 1.5cm (½in) square, a 5cm (2in) square and a 2.5 x 4cm (1 x 1½in) rectangle from the front of the base card as shown.

5 Stick the layered vase and rose image on to the front left-hand side of the card using silicone adhesive. Stick the layered square heart image beneath the square aperture on the inside of the card and repeat for the script-style rectangle. Use a 3D foam pad to stick the stamped heart on to it.

6 Place a flower sticker on to the inside of the card below the small square aperture, and one on to the stamped heart.

Looking into Apertures

Apertures are simply the spaces left behind by cutting 'windows' out of a card. They can be incredibly simple, containing just one cut or punched shape – such as a picture frame – or be more complex multi-apertures. This chapter demonstrates how apertures can produce fun and clever projects such as wonderful shaker cards, or cards with doors that open to reveal surprises. When teamed with the layering and découpage techniques learned in the previous chapter, the three-dimensional quality is extremely eye-catching.

Snowglobe Shaker

This adorable snowman is painted in icy watercolour shades and finished off with sequin snowflakes. Acetate is such a versatile product and is used here with fantastic results to produce a fun card for young and old alike. Other shaker cards can be made the same way for different occasions, for example a stamped image of a bride and groom could be used with horseshoe-shaped confetti for a wedding card.

YOU WILL NEED

See-Ds 'Snowy Days 50301' stamp set and clear acrylic mounting block • VersaMark™ ink pad • Silver embossing powder • White embossed card 15 x 22cm (5⅞ x 8⅝in) for the base card • White smooth card 10 x 9cm (4 x 3½in) • Blue card 15 x 11cm (5⅞ x 4⅜in) • Purple card 2.5 x 8cm (1 x 3⅛in) • Lilac card 2 x 8cm (¾ x 3⅛in) • Acetate 15 x 11cm (5⅞ x 4⅜in) • Papermania 'Contemporary Christmas' paper 1 x 8cm (⅜ x 3⅛in) • Watercolour paints or pencils in shades of blue and purple • Sequins • 3D foam pads • Double-sided tape

FINISHED SIZE 15 x 10.5cm (5⅞ x 4⅛in)

1 Use the VersaMark™ ink pad to carefully ink the snowman stamp, ensuring that the rubber is evenly coated. Stamp the image on to the smooth white card.

2 Sprinkle silver embossing powder over the stamped image and tap off the excess powder, returning it to the container. Remove any stray powder with a paint brush. Heat with the heat gun until the powder melts.

3 Use watercolour paints or pencils to colour the snowman. Once dry, trim around the edge leaving a narrow border.

4 Fold the piece of white embossed card in half to make the base card. Use the template on page 118 to trace the card and aperture shapes on to the base card and then cut them out.

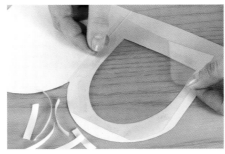

5 Place the shaped base card face down. Trim the acetate to slightly larger than the aperture and then stick it on to the inside left-hand side of the card over the aperture using double-sided tape.

6 Attach 3D foam pads on to the acetate following the shape of the aperture ensuring that they can't be seen from the front and that there are no gaps for the sequins to escape through. Place the snowman on to the acetate towards the bottom of the aperture. Place 3D foam pads on to the back of the snowman. Wipe the acetate with antistatic cloth then sprinkle sequins around the snowman, taking care to keep them away from the foam pads.

stamp smart

Using a coloured un-patterned background, such as this blue, helps to show up the sequins. You can buy snowflake-shaped confetti sequins from craft suppliers, or could use a small snowflake punch to make your own from white card or paper.

7 Using double-sided tape, stick a piece of blue card over the entire inside of the left-hand side of the card and trim around the edge following the card shape.

8 Layer the strip of patterned paper on to the lilac card and then on to the purple card using double-sided tape, and then secure on to the front of the card to finish.

Trick or Treat

The apertures in this project are punched from card, which is then layered. The layers of the card are placed at angles to each other to add drama. Punching or die cutting are the simplest ways to make apertures. Here, a circular punch complements the stamped circles, to create a unique Halloween card.

YOU WILL NEED

Hero Arts® 'Halloween LL708' stamps • Hero Arts® 'Box of Dots LL890' stamps • StazOn® black ink pad • ColorBox® 'Tangerine' and 'Lime' pigment ink pads • Two pieces of white card, one 13 x 26cm (5⅛ x 10¼in) for the base card, and one 7.5cm (3in) square • Orange card 9cm (3½in) square • Lime-green card 11cm (4⅜in) square • Black card 8cm (3⅛in) square • Circular punch approximately 2cm (¾in) in diameter • Black ribbon 14cm (5½in) in length • 3D foam pads • Glue stick

FINISHED SIZE 13cm (5⅛in) square

1 Stamp the large dot twice in Tangerine and twice in Lime ink on to the small square of white card. Stamp the Halloween images using the black ink pad directly over the top of the coloured dots.

2 Use the punch to cut out the two diagonal orange dots. Use 3D foam pads to stick the white card to the black card. Glue the punched dots on to the black card directly underneath where they were punched out, so that they appear recessed.

3 Fold the large piece of white card in half to make the base card.

4 Glue the orange card on to the lime-green card at an angle. Glue the ribbon on top of the layered card securing at the back.

5 Glue the lime-green card centrally on to the front of the base card. Glue the layered black card on to the front of the base card at an angle to finish.

DESIGNER DAISY

Clear embossing powder and VersaMark™ ink are used to stamp this image on to a Stampbord™ tile. The tile is then painted using acrylic paints in fresh colours and allowed to dry before being layered on to coloured card. Smaller stamped tiles are stuck on to the inside of the card, which is covered in orange card so that it shows through the aperture. *Stamps used: Magenta 'Spring Passion'.*

stamp smart

To accurately align the punch over the stamped circle, turn the punch upside down. This way you can see exactly which part of the image you are punching out.

Crockery Cupboard

The doors of this cupboard open to reveal pretty teacups. Ink is applied directly to the paper and the resist embossing technique using clear powder complements the soft colour scheme. Brads are used to make tiny handles to complete the card.

stamp smart
You could cut out some of the pattern from the cupboard doors to resemble fretwork. The doors could also open to reveal a message instead of the cups.

YOU WILL NEED

Inkadinkado Stamps 'Tin Can Mail 92676.X' • Hampton Arts 'C84267 Clear Expressions' stamps and clear acrylic mounting block • VersaMark™ ink pad • ColorBox® 'Lavender', 'Sea Glass' and 'Aqua' pigment ink pads • Clear embossing powder • Three pieces of white card, one 21 x 14.5cm (8¼ x 5¾in) for the base card, and two 10 x 14cm (4 x 5½in) • Two large blue brads • Glue stick

FINISHED SIZE 10.5 x 14.5cm (4⅛ x 5¾in)

1 Use the VersaMark™ ink pad to stamp the image on to the left-hand side of one of the smaller pieces of white card.

2 Use the clear embossing powder to heat emboss the image. Repeat the process on the right-hand side so that the two images are side by side.

3 Use the coloured ink pads to apply the ink directly to the stamped images in a swirling motion (see page 113). Wipe off the excess with a tissue and the embossed image will appear.

4 With a sharp craft knife cut the images close to the outline at the top and bottom and down the centre in between the images. Do not cut the right and left edges. Score down the left and right edges with a ruler and embossing tool or bone folder, and fold the doors back so that they open. Add a brad to each door to represent handles.

5 Fold the large piece of white card in half to make the base card and stick the doors on to the front by applying glue around the narrow border only, so that the doors will open.

6 Using the coloured ink pads, stamp the teacups twice on to the remaining piece of white card and cut around the edges. Cut a 0.5cm (¼in) strip from the same piece of card and apply the inks as before. Glue inside the cupboard to resemble a shelf.

7 Glue the teacups on to the shelf and the bottom of the cupboard to finish.

Fun Flower

The eye-catching aperture for this card is made by cutting flaps from the front of the base card and folding them out, then securing them with brads. The effect is exaggerated by covering the inside of the card with contrasting paper. A circular foam pad is combined with glitter to add sparkle to the central flower motif, but a large brad could be used instead.

1 Use the black ink pad to stamp the image on to all three small pieces of patterned paper. Carefully cut around the outline of each image.

2 Layer together using 3D foam pads. Stick a circular foam pad in to the centre of the top layer, remove the sticky top backing paper and sprinkle the glitter over it. Return the excess glitter to the container.

3 Fold the white card in half to make the base card. Cover the front with patterned paper from the kit and the inside left-hand side with a contrasting paper.

4 Using a soft pencil, faintly draw a 6cm (2⅜in) square on to the inside left-hand side of the base card. Draw two diagonal lines across from corner to corner. Use a sharp craft knife and ruler cut along each diagonal line to make four flaps.

5 Score along the edges of the square with an embossing tool or bone folder, then fold each flap outwards on to the front of the card and secure with a brad at each corner.

6 Glue the layered flower on to the inside of the card centrally beneath the aperture. Erase any remaining pencil lines.

stamp smart
Rather than covering the base card with patterned paper, using coloured card that has a different shade on the reverse (such as Duplex) will achieve similar results.

YOU WILL NEED
Funstamps '3D Flower 2' • StazOn® black ink pad • White card 14.5 x 21cm (5¾ x 8¼in) for the base card • Papermania 'Pastel Paper Kit' printed paper, two pieces 14.5 x 10.5cm (5¾ x 4⅛in), and three pieces 6cm (2⅜in) square • Circular foam pad • 3D foam pads • Pink glitter • Four metal brads • Double-sided tape or glue stick

FINISHED SIZE 14.5 x 10.5cm (5¾ x 4⅛in)

Shuttered Window

This simple stamp has a rustic Mediterranean feel to it and is combined with Flower Soft™ for a quick and clever 3D flower effect. To achieve a slightly different, more vibrant result, colour the shutters pink or even red and choose contrasting Flower Soft™ in bolder colours.

YOU WILL NEED

Great Impressions 'Window' stamp • StazOn® black ink pad • Cream card 15 x 21cm (5⅞ x 8¼in) for the base card • Flower Soft™ • Watercolour paints or pens in shades of blue and brown • General-purpose tacky craft glue

FINISHED SIZE 15 x 10.5cm (5⅞ x 4⅛in)

1 Fold the cream card in half to make a base card. Using the black ink pad, stamp the image centrally on to the front of the base card. Colour the image with the paints or pens.

2 Carefully cut around the top, bottom and centre of the shutters so that they open.

3 Apply dabs of glue along the window box and sprinkle the Flower Soft™ on to the wet glue. Leave to dry flat.

Stained Glass Window

Stamping on acetate teamed with ultra-fine glitter produces a stained glass window effect, created by the light reflecting through the aperture on to the glitter. The image could also be coloured using peel-off markers or overhead projector pens.

YOU WILL NEED

Inca Stamps 'Daisy Stained Glass' • StazOn® black ink pad • Cream card 14 x 28cm (5½ x 11in) for the base card • Acetate 10cm (4in) square • Fine glitter in pink, white, blue and green • Art Glitter Adhesive and fine-tip applicator • Blue ribbon 50cm (20in) in length • Double-sided tape

FINISHED SIZE 14cm (5½in) square

1 Use the black ink pad to stamp the image on to the acetate. Take care not to slide the stamp or the image will smudge. Turn the acetate over and apply the Art Glitter Adhesive to the reverse of the image using the fine-tip applicator. Add the glue and glitter to one area at a time, returning any excess glitter to its container as you work. Allow to dry completely.

2 Fold the cream card in half to make the base card. Cut an 8cm (3⅛in) square from the front of the base card and with the card open place face down on to the work surface. Stick double-sided tape around all four sides of the aperture, then position the acetate centrally face down on top.

3 Tie the ribbon around the front left-hand side of the base card to finish.

Assorted Shapes

Shaped cards are great fun and although they take a little longer to make than conventional single-fold cards, the results are worth the extra effort. Cards can be made in an almost endless variety of shapes and sizes and then be combined with 3D elements such as layering, découpage and embellishments. A shaped card will open and stand as long as the fold line is kept intact, so careful thought is needed prior to cutting out the shape. There are many templates on the market specially designed for making shaped cards, as well as ready-made shaped cards in a rainbow of different colours.

Garden Shed

This is a wonderful card for anyone that enjoys gardening. Not only is the card shaped, but has an opening door and 3D découpage gardener for extra impact. Scrapbook papers are used to make the shed, and the stamped figure is painted using watercolours.

YOU WILL NEED

Paper Nation 'Garden Man PN00' stamp • VersaMark™ ink pad • Black embossing powder • Sandylion scrapbook paper 'Denim Wash' 8.5 x 5cm (3⅜ x 2in) and 'Corduroy' 13 x 9cm (5⅛ x 3½in) • Three pieces of white card, one 13 x 21cm (5⅛ x 8¼in) for the base card, and two 9cm (3½in) square • Watercolour paints or pencils in red, yellow, blue, brown, grey and green • 3D foam pads • Glue stick

FINISHED SIZE 13 x 10.5cm (5⅛ x 4⅛in)

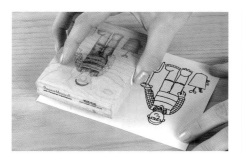

1 Use the VersaMark™ ink pad to carefully ink the stamp, ensuring that the rubber is evenly coated. Stamp the image on to one of the small pieces of white card.

2 Sprinkle black embossing powder over the stamped image and tap off the excess powder, returning it to the container. Remove any stray powder with a paint brush. Heat with the heat gun until the powder melts. Repeat so that there are two complete stamped and embossed images.

3 Colour both images in exactly the same way and once dry, trim around the edge of the first image as close to the embossed outline as possible without cutting or chipping it.

4 Cut the head, collar and boots from the second image and stick directly above the first image using 3D foam pads. Cut out one of the flowerpots and leave to one side.

5 Enlarge the template on page 119 by 50% on a photocopier and use it to trace and cut out a shed shape from the Corduroy paper. Draw an 8 x 4cm (3⅛ x 1½in) rectangle on to the reverse to make the door. Cut around the left, top and bottom edges only and carefully score down the right edge with an embossing tool or bone folder to create a door that opens.

6 Glue the Denim Wash paper behind the door taking care not to get any glue on the door, so that it still opens.

7 Fold the large piece of white card in half to make the base card. Paint the bottom and sides green, then glue the shed on to the front. Glue the layered figure on to the right-hand side of the card in front of the shed. Use a 3D foam pad to stick the plant pot on to the front of the card to the left of the door.

8 Trim around the edges of the base card carefully following the outline of the shed and figure to finish.

stamp smart

Why not place cut out stamped images of tools and plant pots on to the background paper inside the shed? Or a photo fastener could be attached with a brad to 'lock' the shed door, providing a secret place for a special message.

Gentleman's Shirt

This card features a man's shirt and tie and can be presented in its own colourful gift box. The shirt and tie are mounted on to a small base card that can be removed from the box and displayed independently. Real buttons add a life-like detail and an extra 3D touch.

YOU WILL NEED

Funstamps 'Gent's Shirt' • VersaMark™ ink pad • Black embossing powder • Three pieces of KI Memories® 'My Guy' scrapbook paper, one 11 x 16cm (4⅜ x 6¼in) (brown patterned) for the mini base card, one 11 x 8cm (4⅜ x 3⅛in) (white spotted), and one 13.5 x 10.5cm (5⅜ x 4⅛in) (brown patterned) for the box • Two pieces of white card, one 11 x 8cm (4⅜ x 3⅛in) and one 13.5 x 10.5cm (5⅜ x 4⅛in) for the box • Two pieces of blue card 11 x 8cm (4⅜ x 3⅛in) • Four small white buttons • 3D foam pads • Double-sided tape or glue stick

FINISHED SIZE 11 x 8cm (4⅜ x 3⅛in)

1 Use the VersaMark™ ink pad to stamp the image on to the blue card.

2 Use the black embossing powder to heat emboss the image. Repeat the process using the second piece of blue card, one piece of the white card and the white spotted paper.

3 Cut the collar and cuffs from the white card, the pocket from the second piece of blue card and the tie from the white spotted paper. Use 3D foam pads to stick the layers together. Glue the buttons on to the collar, cuff and pocket.

4 Fold the large piece of brown patterned paper in half to make a mini base card and stick the finished shirt on top.

5 Following the instructions in the panel right, make a small box and place the card inside. Decorate the box with a tiny tag to finish.

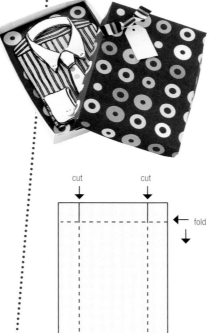

cut   cut

fold

cut   cut

Make the base a fraction smaller
Cut along the solid lines
Fold along the dotted lines

MAKING A BOX

1 Measure the size of the finished card and add 2.5cm (1in) to the top and bottom to determine the size of the card required. Cut two pieces the same size. Here, the white card is used for the base, with the brown patterned paper for the lid.

2 Take the lid piece and with a ruler and embossing tool or bone folder score a line 1cm (⅜in) in from the edge and parallel to each of the four sides.

3 With scissors carefully snip on the two long edges, only up to where the fold lines intersect, and then fold along the scored lines on all four sides.

4 Secure the folded flaps with double-sided tape or glue to complete the lid.

5 Take the base piece of card and carefully trim 3 or 4mm (⅛in) from the top and left-hand side only. Then follow the instructions for making the lid to make the base in the same way. Because the base is slightly smaller the lid should fit comfortably over the top.

Newborn Pram

A square card is rounded at the edges and the top right quarter cut away to make a simple pram or crib shape. Scrapbook paper decorates the base card, but baby-themed images could be stamped on to it instead. Change the colour scheme for a girl by using pink papers and ink. Alternatively use yellows and pale greens for a unisex design.

stamp smart
Try punching two circles to make wheels and adding a handle cut from a strip embellished with other baby-themed items, such as a real nappy (diaper) pin.

YOU WILL NEED
Anita's 'Rattle' stamp • Brilliance 'Sky Blue' pigment ink pad • Sandylion scrapbook paper 'Baby Blue Stripes' 13cm (5⅛in) square, and two strips of 'Baby Blue Dots' 2.5 x 15cm (1 x 5⅞in) • Three pieces of white card, one 13 x 26cm (5⅛ x 10¼in) for the base card, and two 1.5 x 8cm (½ x 3⅛in) • Papermania metal rimmed tag • Narrow blue ribbon 20cm (8in) in length • Tiny button • Tiny silver punched heart • Wavy-edged scissors • 3D foam pads • Glue stick

FINISHED SIZE 13cm (5⅛in) square

1 Use the blue ink pad to stamp the image on to the tag. Punch a small hole out of the tag and tie a length of the ribbon through it, securing it with a bow. Glue the silver heart and button on to the tag as shown.

2 Fold the large piece of white card in half to make the base card. Use the template on page 118 to trace the shape on to the front of the card using a soft pencil and cut out following the outline carefully.

3 Cover the front of the card with the Baby Blue Stripes paper. Fold the strips of Baby Blue Dots paper into pleats and glue along the edges of the pram.

4 Use the wavy-edged scissors to cut along one edge of both the strips of white card. Glue on to the edge of the base card over the pleats. Glue the remaining lengths of ribbon on top.

5 Use a 3D foam pad to stick the tag on to the card where the two strips of pleated paper meet.

Bright Bouquet

A shop-bought triangle card is decorated with
bold papers and a contemporary stamp to produce
a cheerful and highly unusual card. The generic
nature of this card means it can be used for
any occasion, from a simple thank you,
to birthday wishes, or even get well soon.
Here, the other sides of the card are left
plain, but they could be decorated with
stamps or patterned paper to enhance
the 3D aspect even more.

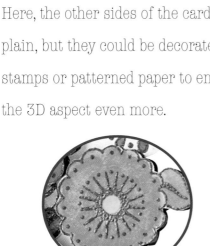

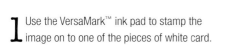

1 Use the VersaMark™ ink pad to stamp the
image on to one of the pieces of white card.

2 Use the gold embossing to heat emboss the
image. Repeat the process on the second
piece of white card.

3 Colour both images with the paints or pencils,
and trim around the edges of the first image.
Cut out the flowers from the second image and
layer on to the first using 3D foam pads.

4 Take the square of CC-04 paper, fold the left
and bottom side inwards so that they overlap
and make a rough triangle shape. Glue the top
edge down. Glue the stamped flowers inside to
make the bouquet.

5 Assemble the triangle card, cover the front
with the strip of CC-01 paper. Secure the
eyelets on the front and back so they lie next to
each other when the card is closed. Tie the ribbon
through both eyelets and finish with a bow.

stamp smart
**Add extra layers and bright adhesive
gems or beads in the centres of the
flowers for greater impact. A mini tag
complete with message could also be
added to finish the bouquet.**

YOU WILL NEED
Elusive Images 'Vase of Flowers Stitch'n'Stamp' • VersaMark™ ink pad • Gold embossing powder • MMBI paper 'CC-01' 4 x 11cm (1½ x 4⅜in) and 'CC-04'
9cm (3½in) square • Two pieces of white card 10cm (4in) square • Papermania white triangle base card • Green ribbon 30cm (12in) in length • Two gold
eyelets • Paints or coloured pencils in pink, yellow, orange and green • 3D foam pads • Glue stick

FINISHED SIZE 14 x 12cm (5½ x 4¾in)

Christmas Cracker

This simple shape is instantly recognizable as a festive cracker. A gold base card is folded at the top and a template is traced on to it. The card is stamped and heat embossed with gold embossing powder to create an almost dry-embossed appearance.

YOU WILL NEED

Rubbadubbadoo 'Poinsettia' stamp • Hero Arts® 'Florentine Scroll Background' stamp • VersaMark™ ink pad • Gold embossing powder • Three pieces of gold card, one 16 x 22cm (6¼ x 8⅝in) for the base card, and two strips 1.5 x 8cm (½ x 3⅛in) • Red card 8cm (3⅛in) square • Green card 6.5cm (2½in) square • Green ribbon 30cm (12in) in length • Gold thread 1m (3ft) in length • Peel-off gold dots (or circles punched from gold card) • Deckle-edged scissors • Glue stick

FINISHED SIZE 7.5 x 21cm (3 x 8¼in)

1 Fold the large piece of gold card in half to make the base card. Enlarge the template on page 119 by 50% on a photocopier, then carefully trace the outline on to the front of the base card. Cut around the edge of the outline leaving the fold line intact.

2 Use the VersaMark™ ink pad to stamp the Florentine Scroll image on to the front of the base card.

3 Use the gold embossing powder to heat emboss the image.

4 Use the same ink and embossing powder to stamp and heat emboss the Poinsettia on to the red card. Trim around the edges and layer on to the green card. Glue on to the front of the base card.

5 Use the deckle-edged scissors to cut the edges of both strips of gold card. Glue on to the base card at the narrowest points of the cracker. Wrap the ribbon first and then the gold thread several times around the base card.

6 Decorate the left and right edges of the base card with a row of peel-off dots or punched gold circles to finish.

AUTUMN LEAVES

The sides of this card are folded so that they meet in the middle and open to make a gatefold card. The front has a decorated panel made using a leaf stamp and gold embossing powder on coloured card. The inside of the card is decorated by stamping the image using VersaMark™ ink and applying coloured chalk with a cotton wool ball gently over the top so as not to smudge the ink. The papers complement the autumnal theme of the card. *Stamps used: Chapel Road Art Stamps 'Pear' and Hero Arts® 'Leaves'.*

Pretty Purse

Bright turquoise and greens are used to make this fun card, and stamped tags add the finishing touches. Punches are great for making quick and inexpensive embellishments for a card. For a more traditional feel, use softer colours or antique-styled patterned papers.

1 Use the VersaMark™ ink pad and silver embossing powder to stamp and heat emboss the handbag on to the blue pearlescent card. Trim around the edge. Repeat using the background stamp on to the square of aqua card. Punch out the dress shape from the stamped aqua card.

2 Enlarge the template on page 119 by 50% on a photocopier, then trace and cut out the handbag shape from the large piece of aqua card. Fold the card in half along the fold line to make the base card. Layer the bright green pearlescent card on to the dark green pearlescent card, then glue or tape across the centre of the handbag.

3 Cut the top corners from the pieces of white card to make tag shapes. Pierce the tops of two of the tags with a sharp needle and thread the ribbon through. Tie to make a bow. Use 3D foam pads to stick the tags to the front of the base card.

4 Punch two shoes from the leftover scraps of blue card and stick on to one of the tags. Stick the stamped handbag and dress on to the other two tags with glue or double-sided tape.

5 Glue the sequins on to the handbag and shoes and the rosebud on to the dress to complete the card.

stamp smart
You could use any background stamp to make the pattern for the dress. The handbag base card could be stamped with the same background stamp; the same applies to the strips of green pearlescent card.

YOU WILL NEED
Inkadinkado Stamps '95392-G' • Aspects of Design 'Daisy Daydreams' stamp sheet and clear acrylic mounting block • VersaMark™ ink pad • Silver embossing powder • Bright green pearlescent card 16 x 3cm (6¼ x 1⅛in) • Dark green pearlescent card 16 x 4cm (6¼ x 1½in) • Three pieces of white pearlescent card 4 x 2cm (1½ x ¾in) • Blue pearlescent card 7 x 5cm (2¾ x 2in) • Two pieces of aqua card, one 18 x 28cm (7 x 11in) for the base card, and one 5cm (2in) square • Woodware 'Shoe' and '2in Dress' punches • Narrow blue ribbon 20cm (8in) in length • Three blue sequins • White fabric rosebud • 3D foam pads • Glue stick or double-sided tape

FINISHED SIZE 14.5 x 14cm (5¾ x 5½in)

Holiday Memories

This concertina-folded card makes a great mini album and is a fun way to display your favourite photos. The colour scheme of aqua and blue reflects the holiday theme, and simple shell stamps and 3D embellishments add to its impact.

stamp smart

Change the photographs, colours and embellishments to suit the occasion. The theme could just as easily be Merry Christmas or Welcome Baby, both of which would make lovely gifts to family members.

YOU WILL NEED

Hero Arts® 'Ornamental Shells LL732' stamps • Inkadinkado Stamps 'Tin Can Mail 91662-Y' • PSX 'D-190' shell stamp • VersaMark™ ink pad • Clear embossing powder • KI Memories® scrapbook papers 22 x 10cm (8⅝ x 4in) and 17 x 10cm, (6⅝ x 4in) • Magenta scrapbook paper 17 x 10cm (6⅝ x 4in), 3.5 x 10cm (1⅜ x 4in), 3 x 10cm (1⅛ x 4in) • Two pieces of blue card, one 15 x 8.5cm (5⅞ x 3⅜in), and one 4.5 x 10cm (1¾ x 4in) • Two pieces of pale aqua card, one 15 x 10cm (5⅞ x 4in), and one 5 x 10cm (2 x 4in) • Three pieces of mid-aqua card, one 14 x 10cm (5½ x 4in), and two 7cm (2¾in) square • Two pieces of deep aqua card, one 8.5 x 7cm (3⅜ x 2¾in), and one 11 x 9cm (4⅜ x 3½in) • Two pieces of lemon card, one 4 x 10cm (1½ x 4in), and one 7 x 10cm (2¾ x 4in) • Five pieces of white card, one 21 x 29.7cm (8¼ x 11⅝in), one 14 x 9cm (5½ x 3½in), one 8 x 6.5cm (3⅛ x 2½in), and two 6cm (2⅜in) square • Watercolour paints in blue and green • Dress It Up buttons • EK Success 'Epoxy Seashore Tokens' • Paint swatch • Five brads • Three photographs • Glue stick or double-sided tape

FINISHED SIZE 21 x 10cm (8¼ x 4in)

1 Take the large piece of white card, score and fold 9.9cm (3⅞in) from the left and right edges to make a zigzag or concertina-folded base card. Unfold and lay flat. Draw a diagonal line measuring 14cm (5½in) up from the bottom on the left-hand edge and 21cm (8¼in) up from the bottom on the right-hand edge. Cut across the diagonal line.

2 Cover the three inside sections using the patterned scrapbook paper on the right and left sides and the lemon and mid-aqua card in the centre. Tear the bottom of the mid-aqua card so that the white chamfered edge is visible (see page 116) before gluing it on to the lemon card.

3 Cover the front with the Magenta paper and strips of blue and pale aqua card. Cover the back section with the pale aqua, blue and lemon card as shown.

4 Decorate the pages by layering photos on top of the deep aqua card and adding the embellishments with glue or double-sided tape.

5 Use the VersaMark™ ink pad and clear embossing powder to stamp and heat emboss the images. Apply the watercolour paints and allow them to mix together before layering on to coloured card and arrange as shown.

Playful Pop-Ups

Pop-ups bring a wealth of 3D fun to your paper projects and are always a big hit with children. Often the pop-up is a surprise, only revealed when the card is opened. Pop-ups can consist of simple tabs or a more complicated tiered mechanism that tells a story. Other types of pop-ups can be made by cutting out shapes directly on the fold line. However you create your pop-ups, they are sure to bring delight to whoever receives them.

Birthday Balloons

This bright birthday card is decorated with patterned paper; the balloons are stamped on to matching card and appear to be popping out of a gift. Use as many balloons as you wish – just stamp the image on to scraps of coloured card and attach silver coiled wire before sticking them to the inside of the card. Slits are made in the base card to make the pop-up feature.

1 Fold the white card in half to make the base card. Fold the large piece of scrapbook paper in half and measuring 6cm (2⅜in) up from the bottom make a 6cm (2⅜in) horizontal slit across the fold line.

YOU WILL NEED

HobbyCraft '43123HC Balloons' stamp • VersaMark™ ink pad • Black embossing powder • White card 14.5 x 20cm (5¾ x 7⅞in) for the base card • Yellow, blue and red card, one piece of each 5cm (2in) square • Two pieces of ProvoCraft 'Rob and Bob Studio' scrapbook paper, one 14.5 x 20cm (5¾ x 7⅞in) (numbers), and one 6cm (2⅜in) square (stripes) • Spool of thin silver wire • Cocktail stick • Narrow pink ribbon 15cm (6in) in length • 3D foam pads • Glue stick

2 Fold the paper and crease at the left and right side where the slit ends. This will make a tab that pops up once the card is open.

3 Cut slits 4.5cm (1¾in) and 5.5cm (2⅛in) down from the top of the patterned paper making the slits about 4.5cm (1¾in) wide; this will make a tab for the balloons.

4 Glue the patterned paper on to the base card but do not put glue on the pop-up parts, otherwise they will not pop up. Glue the square piece of scrapbook paper on to the pop-up box. Decorate with the ribbon tied into a bow.

5 Use the VersaMark™ ink pad to carefully stamp the balloon image on to the yellow card. Use the black embossing powder to heat emboss the image. Repeat with the red and blue card. Cut the balloons out and layer one red and one blue balloon on to the yellow balloons with 3D foam pads.

6 Cut 6cm (2⅜in) lengths of wire and loosely wrap around a cocktail stick, remove from the stick and secure on to the reverse of the stamped balloons with 3D foam pads.

7 Glue the balloons on the inside of the card. Glue the yellow layered balloons on to the slit. Decorate the front of the card with patterned paper.

stamp smart

Use a solvent ink to stamp images on to actual balloons. When the balloon is blown up the image will enlarge. Try stamping on partially blown up balloons to vary the size of the images. Peel-off markers or overhead projector pens can then be used to colour the images.

Beautiful Box

The stamp used here is very clever and features a fold line so that once the stamped box is folded and assembled the lid can pop-up to reveal a hidden message or object.

YOU WILL NEED

Limited Edition Stamps 'The Surprise Package LE6119' • VersaMark™ ink pad • Black embossing powder • Paper Adventures scrapbook paper 'Primavera Dots' 14 x 13cm (5½ x 5⅛in), and 'Peachy Shadow Wash' 10.5 x 14.5cm (4⅛ x 5¾in) • Two pieces of pink card 14 x 13cm (5½ x 5⅛in) plus a scrap • White card 21 x 14.5cm (8¼ x 5¾in) for the base card • Tissue paper 10 x 20cm (4 x 8in) • Small heart punch • Black pen • 3D foam pads • Glue stick

FINISHED SIZE 10.5 x 14.5cm (4⅛ x 5¾in)

1 Use the VersaMark™ ink pad to stamp the image on to the Primavera Dots paper.

2 Use the black embossing powder to heat emboss the image. Repeat this process on the two pieces of pink card and set aside.

3 Cut out the image on the Dots paper and fold along the marked lines. Glue scrunched up tissue paper under the lid.

4 Cut out the ribbon and bow from one of the images stamped on the pink card, and just the bow from the other piece. Glue the ribbon on to the box, then layer the bow on to the present using 3D foam pads.

5 Cut a simple tag shape from a scrap of pink card and add a punched heart. Use a black pen to add a border and kisses.

6 Fold the white card in half to make the base card. Cover the front with the Peachy Shadow Wash paper. Glue the completed gift box on top.

UP AND AWAY

The balloon image here is stamped on to the centre of the card before cutting around the top and folding in half. This is a great way to achieve a pop-up effect without having to cut slits or make tabs, and makes a fun place setting card for a children's party. Vary the theme to produce place settings suitable for any occasion. *Stamp used: Funstamps 'Big Balloon'.*

Petal Envelope

The 3D element of this invitation card is two-fold, firstly the envelope can be opened to reveal a pop-up centre layered on to a small base card, which can then be opened further to reveal the message. A tab is made by folding a strip of paper or card into a rough four-sided open box, which allows the centre stamped image to pop-up and then lay flat when the envelope is closed.

1 Enlarge the template on page 119 by 50% on a photocopier. Use it to trace and cut out the shape from the large square of striped paper.

2 Fold the rectangular piece of green paper in half and stick the back piece to the centre of the inside of the envelope. Write the sentiment or message on the inside of the green paper.

3 Using the VersaMark™ ink pad and purple embossing powder, stamp and heat emboss the circular stamp on to the square of pink paper and trim around the edge close to the outline. Glue on to the centre of the green folded paper.

4 Stamp and heat emboss the circular rose and four corner stamps on to the pieces of white card also using the VersaMark™ ink pad and purple embossing powder, then trim around the edges. Paint the stamped images and glue the four corner pieces on to the inside of the envelope.

5 Fold the strip of white card 1.5cm (½in) in from each end, and then again 3cm (1⅛in) from each end. Bend around the two edges and glue together to make a square tab. Glue the bottom of the tab to the centre of the pink stamped circle and the top of the tab to the underneath side of the painted rose. When the envelope is closed the rose will lie flat; when opened it will pop-up.

YOU WILL NEED

Elusive Images 'Rose Mandala' stamp set and clear acrylic mounting block • VersaMark™ ink pad • Purple embossing powder • Three pieces of Papermania 'Pastel Embellishment Kit' paper, one 21cm (8¼in) square (stripes), one 10 x 20cm (4 x 8in) (green), and one 10cm (4in) square (pink) • Six pieces of white card, one 10cm (4in) square, four 6cm (2⅜in) square, and one 1 x 7.5cm (⅜ x 3in) • Watercolour paints in pink, yellow and green • Glue stick

FINISHED SIZE 10cm (4in) square

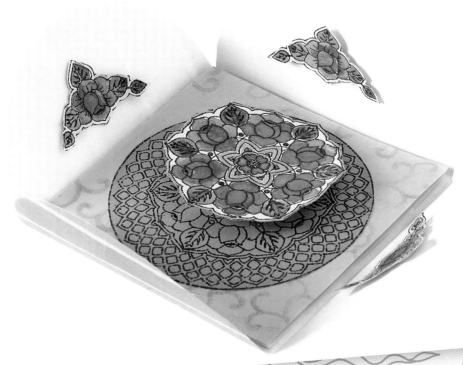

Tumbling Hedgehogs

This stamp is perfect for a cascading waterfall-style card as it tells a story, which is revealed as the tab is pulled downwards. The waterfall mechanism could also be used to show themed images instead of using a story stamp.

YOU WILL NEED

Penny Black 'A Great Surprise' stamp • StazOn® black ink pad • White card 6 x 16cm (2⅜ x 6¼in) • Three pieces of green card 6cm (2⅜in) square • Yellow card 7.5 x 7cm (3 x 2¾in) • Two pieces of blue card, one 1.5 x 11.5cm (½ x 4½in), and one 13 x 1.5cm (5⅛ x ½in) • Red card 22 x 4cm (8⅝ x 1½in) • Crafty Bitz 'BC53W' embossed single-fold base card • Watercolour paints in pink, grey, blue, green and purple • Glue stick

FINISHED SIZE 17 x 11.5cm (6⅝ x 4½in)

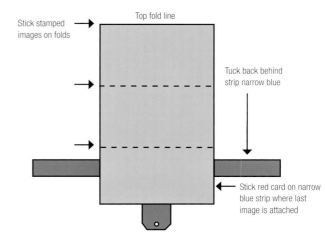

Stick stamped images on folds

Top fold line

Tuck back behind strip narrow blue

Stick red card on narrow blue strip where last image is attached

1 Using the black ink pad, stamp the image on to the white card. Trim each section to make three 5cm (2in) squares with the image centrally on each. Colour with the paints. Layer the images on to the pieces of green card.

2 Fold the red card 11cm (4⅜in) from the top, 13.5cm (5⅜in) from the top, 4.5cm (1¾in) from the bottom and 7.5cm (3in) from the bottom.

3 Glue the layered bottom image on to the red card so that the top of it lies across the bottom fold line (4.5cm/1¾in from the bottom). Glue the second image so that it lies on top of the first with the top edge in line across the next fold line up (7.5cm/3in from the bottom). Glue the first image so that it lies on top of the second with the top edge lying across the top fold line (13.5cm/5⅜in from the top).

4 Glue the yellow card centrally on to the base card. Stick the smaller blue strip across the base card, beneath the yellow card. Ensure that the strip is stuck at the edges only otherwise the mechanism won't work.

5 Fold the red card in half so that the three mounted images are at the front. Tuck the back piece behind the blue strip that was stuck on to the base card in step 4. Glue the long strip of blue card on to the red card so that it lies on the underside of the top folded top section (the part where the mounted images are attached). Allow the strip to protrude about 2cm (¾in) below the stamped images and trim the sides to make a simple tag shape.

6 Stick the underneath side of the red card where the last image is attached on to the horizontal blue strip, this will allow the waterfall mechanism to work when pulling the blue tab in a downward motion.

Winter Wonderland

The pop-up elements of the snowman and bushes in the foreground on this card are made by folding strips to make small tabs or open boxes, much like the centre tab of the Petal Envelope on page 59. The stamped village scene gives a sense of depth, and is simply coloured using white watercolour paint. Liquid Appliqué creates wonderfully realistic and highly tactile snow.

1 Use the VersaMark™ ink pad to stamp the village scene image on to the large piece of dark blue card.

2 Use the white embossing powder to heat emboss the image. Repeat the process with the tree stamps on to the other two pieces of dark blue card.

3 Stamp the snowman on to the small piece of white card and use the dark blue embossing powder to heat emboss the image. Cut out the trees and snowman, carefully following the outlines.

4 Fold the large piece of white card in half to make the base card. Glue the stamped village scene on to the inside of the base card.

5 Fold one strip of dark blue card 1.5cm (½in) from each end, and then again 3cm (1⅛in) from each end. Bend around the two edges and glue together to make a square tab. Repeat with the second strip of dark blue card.

6 Glue the tabs to the base card, holding the folded card open so that a 90-degree angle is made. Glue the back of the tab on to the vertical side and the bottom of the tab on to the horizontal side. Glue the tree and snowman images on to the front of the tabs. When closed the tabs will lie flat.

7 Apply Liquid Appliqué to the horizontal part of the card and heat according to the manufacturer's instructions so that it puffs up. Allow to cool.

8 Decorate the front of the card with stamped images or scrapbook paper.

YOU WILL NEED

See-Ds 'Snowy Days' stamp sheet and clear acrylic mounting block • Personal Impressions '241 P' stamp • VersaMark™ ink pad • White embossing powder • Dark blue embossing powder • Two pieces of white card, one 21 x 14.5cm (8¼in x 5¾in) for the base card, and one 8 x 5cm (3⅛ x 2in) • Five pieces of dark blue card, one 9.5 x 13.5cm (3¾ x 5⅜in), two 6 x 5cm (2⅜ x 2in), and two strips 1.5 x 7.5cm (½ x 3in) • Watercolour paints in white, blue, red, yellow and green • Liquid Appliqué (white) • Glitter glue • Glue stick

FINISHED SIZE 10.5 x 14.5cm (4⅛ x 5¾in)

Golden Christmas Tree

This sumptuous Christmas card is cut along the fold line similarly to the Up and Away place setting card on page 58 to create the pop-up aspect. A sophisticated palette of gold is used along with sequins and ribbon for a card that will be treasured.

YOU WILL NEED

Hero Arts® 'Florentine Scroll Background' stamp • Hero Arts® 'Long Writing Background' stamp • VersaMark™ ink pad • Gold embossing powder • Cream card 20 x 10cm (8 x 4in) for the base card • Gold card 12 x 10cm (4¾ x 4in) • Vellum 10 x 8cm (4 x 3⅛in) • Sequins • Glitter glue • Narrow gold ribbon 10cm (4in) in length • Fiskars Border punch • Glue stick

FINISHED SIZE 10 x 13.5cm (4 x 5⅜in)

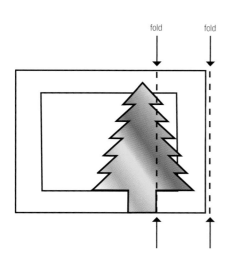

1 Fold the cream card in half to make the base card. Use the VersaMark™ ink pad to stamp the Long Writing Background image on to the inside left-hand side of the base card.

2 Use the gold embossing powder to heat emboss the image.

3 Fold the cream card 7cm (2¾in) from the left-hand side. Trace the tree template on page 118 on to the inside of the card so that the right-hand side of the trunk aligns with the fold line.

4 With a pencil and ruler draw a box 1.5cm (½in) from the top and bottom and 2cm (¾in) from the right and left sides of the front of the card. Cut out the box leaving the traced tree shape intact.

5 Trace the same tree shape on to the gold card and cut out. Use the gold embossing powder and VersaMark™ ink pad to stamp and heat emboss the Florentine Scroll Background image on to the gold tree. Glue on sequins and add dots of glitter glue. Add a bow made from the gold ribbon to the tree trunk and glue on to the base card.

6 Use the gold embossing powder and VersaMark™ ink pad to stamp and heat emboss the Florentine Scroll Background image on to the vellum. Glue on to the right-hand side of the base card.

7 Use the border punch to cut away the right-hand edge of the base card. Carefully fold the left-hand side along the fold line so that the tree protrudes.

Dancing Fairy

This pretty card, perfect for a little girl's birthday, is made using a simple aperture cut from a folded piece of paper which is then glued on to the inside of a base card. The fairy is suspended on silver thread so that she dances, and twinkling fairy dust is created with glitter glue.

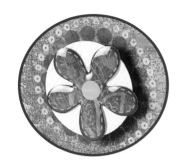

1 Fold the large piece of white card in half to make the base card. Fold the Jumbo Flowers paper in half and then fold again 5cm (2in) left and right from the centre fold.

2 Measure 1.5cm (½in) from top and bottom and then 4.5cm (1¾in) left and right from the centre fold, half way down the paper. Join these points to make a diamond shape and cut out.

3 Place the paper face down and glue the silver cord down the centre fold line.

4 Glue the patterned paper on to the inside of the base card on the left and right parts only so that the centre fold is allowed to fold inwards when closed.

5 Use the brown ink pad to stamp the image on to the white card, trim around the outline and colour the image with the paints. Apply glitter glue to the wings and fairy and down each edge of the card. Stick the fairy to the cord using a piece of tape across the back to secure it.

6 Decorate the front of the closed card with the Atomic Daisies paper and flower stickers.

YOU WILL NEED

Personal Impressions 'P243' stamp • StazOn® 'Timber Brown' ink pad • Sandylion scrapbook paper 'Jumbo Flowers' 25 x 14.5cm (9⅞ x 5¾in), 'Atomic Daisies' 11 x 7.5cm (4⅜ x 3in), and sticker sheet 'Flowers 2' • Two pieces of white card, one 25 x 14.5cm (9⅞ x 5¾in) for the base card, and one 9 x 6.5cm (3½ x 2½in) • Silver cord or thread 14cm (5½in) • Watercolour paints in pink and orange • Glitter glue • Glue stick • Tape

FINISHED SIZE 14.5 x 12.5cm (5¾ x 5in)

Extra-Special Embellishments

One of the easiest ways to add 3D interest to your paper projects and give them a unique twist is to invest in some gorgeous embellishments. Purpose-made craft trimmings include brads, eyelets, buttons, charms and ribbons. As well as these, also consider using natural objects such as leaves, shells and dried flowers. Embellishment is not just about hardware though – decoration can be created by stitching on to parts of the design, or using lacing techniques with rows of eyelets, both of which are inexpensive yet provide a real flourish.

Golfing Days

This simple-to-make desk calendar is embellished using stamped images, page pebbles, peel-offs and rub-on images, together with patterned paper to complete the look. A truly great gift, the calendar could be made using any theme – searching out the embellishments is the best part!

YOU WILL NEED

Inkadinkado Stamps '93875-X' and '93885-K' • VersaMark™ ink pad • Black embossing powder • Making Memories® 'Avenue Collection' embellishment paper 6 x 6in pad • Orange card 10 x 7cm (4 x 2¾in) • Two pieces of white card, one sheet A4 size (29.7 x 21cm / 11⅝ x 8¼in), and one 4cm (1½in) square • Page pebble • Anita's 'Golf' Outline Stickers (silver) • Royal Langnickel Create a Collage 'Golf Collage' Rub-Ons • Small tear-off calendar • 3D foam pads • Glue stick

FINISHED SIZE 10 x 21cm (4 x 8¼in)

1 Use the VersaMark™ ink pad to carefully ink the golf club stamp, ensuring that the rubber is evenly coated. Stamp the golf club image on to the orange card.

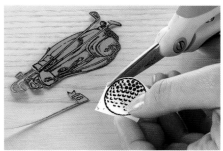

2 Sprinkle black embossing powder over the stamped image and tap off the excess powder, returning it to the jar. Remove stray powder with a paint brush. Heat with the heat gun until the powder melts. Repeat the process with the golf ball image on to the small piece of white card. Trim around the edges of both images carefully following the outline.

3 Make a fold 2.5cm (1in) and another fold 5cm (2in) from each edge of the large piece of white card.

4 Fold the large piece of white card in half and glue pieces of the patterned paper on to the front to create a pleasing design.

5 Glue the stamped golf clubs on to the right-hand side and place a large page pebble over the top of the golf ball image, stick next to the golf clubs using a 3D foam pad.

6 Apply the Rub-Ons to the front of the card, decorate with the Outline Stickers and add the tear-off calendar in the centre.

7 Glue the edges of the card together by overlapping one edge on to the other, carefully aligning the fold lines so that the calendar stands up.

stamp smart

A soft, muted colour scheme complements the nostalgic style of the Rub-Ons used. It also prevents the calendar from looking too busy. If using a bolder colour scheme make sure you choose a simple pattern for the background papers.

Ballet Dreams

Eyelets are attached to this attractive card and then laced with ribbon. Soft pinks and lilacs are used to co-ordinate with the ballet theme. The stamped ballet shoes are given the découpage treatment and then covered with glitter for a touch of magical sparkle.

1 Use the VersaMark™ ink pad to stamp the image on to one of the 8 x 5.5cm (3⅛ x 2⅛in) pieces of scrapbook paper.

2 Use the purple embossing powder to heat emboss the image. Repeat the process with the two other pieces of the same size. Leave the first image intact, cut the shoes and ribbon from the background of the second image and on the third image cut the shoes and ribbon away from the background. Layer the pieces together using 3D foam pads.

3 Fold the white card in half to make the base card. Make a crease and fold the front only about 2.5cm (1in) from the left-hand side. Glue the front to the left of the fold line on to the inside so that it sticks to the back piece.

4 Cover the front of the base card with the remaining pieces of scrapbook paper, as shown. Cut an 8 x 5.5cm (3⅛ x 2⅛in) rectangle out of the front of the base card.

5 Attach the eyelets down the left-hand side of the card, through the front and back so that they are evenly spaced.

6 Starting at the top and working downwards, thread the ribbon up through the first eyelet, down through the second, up through the third, down through the fourth, up through the fifth, and down through the sixth. Bring the ribbon up through the seventh eyelet and then work it through the gaps, tying into a bow at the top.

7 Glue the layered ballet shoes image beneath the aperture on the inside of the card. Add the brads to each corner. Apply glitter glue to the shoes to finish.

YOU WILL NEED
Funstamps 'FM156 Ballet' • VersaMark™ ink pad • Purple embossing powder • Five pieces of Blonde Moments scrapbook paper, one 15 x 8cm (5⅞ x 3⅛in), one 15 x 2.5cm (5⅞ x 1in), and three 8 x 5.5cm (3⅛ x 2⅛in) • White card 15 x 21cm (5⅞ x 8¼in) for the base card • Seven lilac eyelets • Four lilac brads • Lilac ribbon 30cm (12in) in length • Glitter glue • 3D foam pads • Glue stick

FINISHED SIZE 15 x 10.5cm (5⅞ x 4⅛in)

Floral Files

Stamped images combined with stitching and punched shapes make a great focal point for this file folder. Soft muted apricots and lilacs are combined with chalks to give a traditional feel. Piercing the card with a needle to make the holes first makes the stitching much easier.

YOU WILL NEED

Anna Griffiths '580K01' stamp • VersaMark™ ink pad • Two pieces of white card, one 14.5 x 22cm (5¾ x 8⅝in) for the folder, and one 9cm (3½in) square • Three pieces of lilac card in varying shades, one 6cm (2⅜in) square, and two 4cm (1½in) square • For the tabs: peach card 4.5 x 2cm (1¾ x ¾in), tangerine card 9.5 x 2cm (3¾ x ¾in), and lilac card 14 x 2cm (5½ x ¾in) • For the pages: sheets of white paper 14 x 18cm (5½ x 7in) • Shimmer chalks and cotton wool ball • Purple brad • Tiny and small flower punches • Lilac ribbon 50cm (20in) in length • Lilac thread and needle • Glue stick

FINISHED SIZE 14.5 x 11cm (5¾ x 4⅜in)

MAKING FOLDER PAGES AND TABS

To make the inside of the folder, fold the paper pages in half, align with the centre fold of the folder and then open all the pages so they are flat. Using a needle and white thread, stitch long stitches through all the layers on to the fold line, making them about 8cm (3⅛in) long. Tie a knot to secure, then cut the thread as close to the knot as possible. Glue the tabs on to the pages. Start with the smallest tab on top and allow a few pages in between each one.

1 Fold the large piece of white card in half to make the folder. Use the VersaMark™ ink pad to stamp the image on to the front of the card. Apply the chalks to the image using the cotton wool ball (see page 114). Repeat on the small piece of white card without folding it, then cut a 5.5cm (2⅛in) square and punch one small and one tiny flower from the leftover piece.

2 Punch a small flower from the small piece of lilac card. Layer the flowers together and secure the brad in the centre. Glue on to the other small piece of lilac card and stitch around the edge through both layers using a zigzag stitch; add small cross stitches to each corner.

3 Layer the embellished square on to the larger square of lilac card and stick on to the front of the folder. Secure the ribbon around the front left-hand side. Make the inside following the instructions in the panel above.

PARMA VIOLET

A simple card is made from scraps leftover from the main project. The central embellishment is made by punching and layering flower shapes with cross stitches placed in the centre of the petals. The holes are made with a piercing tool or needle prior to stitching. A brad is attached in the centre of the flower to keep the layers in place. *Stamps used: Anna Griffin 'With Gratitude' clear stamp set.*

Beaded Flowers

Seed beads are glued to the centre of these stamped flowers to produce a lovely 3D focal point. This card has a very sophisticated feel, but you can vary the size and colour of the beads depending upon the type of flower used to produce different effects.

YOU WILL NEED

Hero Arts® 'Poetic Petals LL582' and 'Manuscript Background H2141' stamps • StazOn® black ink pad • Brilliance 'Galaxy Gold' pigment ink pad • Three pieces of cream card, one 14 x 28cm (5½ x 11in) for the base card, and two 6cm (2⅜in) square • Burgundy card 14 x 7cm (5½ x 2¾in) • Selection of seed beads • Cream and gold ribbon 30cm (12in) in length • General-purpose tacky craft glue • 3D foam pads

FINISHED SIZE 14cm (5½in) square

1 Fold the large piece of cream card in half to make the base card. Fold the front piece in half again so that the inside is visible and cover with the burgundy card.

2 Use the gold ink pad to stamp the Manuscript Background image twice down the inside right of the card.

3 Use the black ink pad to stamp the flowers on to the smaller pieces of cream card. Cut around the outlines of the flowers

4 Glue the beads in to the centre of the flowers and allow to dry.

5 Glue the ribbon around the folded front of the base card securing it inside the card. Use 3D foam pads to stick the flowers on to the ribbon to finish.

MAJESTIC LION

Beads are used again on this stylish card but this time threaded on to thin wire. Using wooden beads complements the African theme. The image is stamped on to white card that has been coloured with ink using the direct to paper technique (see page 113) and then heat embossed using gold embossing powder. *Stamp used: Stamping Sensations 'INR-028'.*

Natural Charm

A rich cream and gold palette is used with a gold skeleton leaf, paper roses and printed ribbon to produce this exquisite card, suitable for any occasion.

YOU WILL NEED

Hero Arts® 'Manuscript Background H2141' stamp • VersaMark™ ink pad • Gold embossing powder • Three pieces of white card, one A4 size (29.7 x 21cm / 11⅝ x 8¼in) for the base card, one 14 x 9cm (5½ x 3½in), and one 6 x 10.5cm (2⅜ x 4⅛in) • Cream embossed card 10.5 x 7cm (4⅛in x 2¾in) • Gold skeleton leaf • Patterned gold ribbon 6cm (2⅜in) wide x 17cm (6⅝in) long • Narrow gold ribbon 30cm (12in) in length • Three paper rosebuds • Skeleton leaf • General-purpose tacky craft glue • Glue stick

FINISHED SIZE 21 x 15cm (8¼ x 5⅞in)

1 Use the VersaMark™ ink pad to stamp the image on to the 14 x 9cm (5½ x 3½in) piece of white card.

2 Use the gold embossing powder to heat emboss the image.

3 Fold the large piece of white card in half to make the base card. Glue the cream embossed card on to the bottom right-hand side of the stamped background image and tie a length of the narrow ribbon around both layers. Glue centrally on to the front of the base card.

4 Wrap the wide ribbon around the remaining piece of white card and secure at the back. Glue on to the top left-hand side of the stamped layered background.

5 Use the tacky craft glue to stick the skeleton leaf carefully on to the ribbon. Tie the paper roses and leaf with the remaining narrow ribbon and stick on to the skeleton leaf to finish.

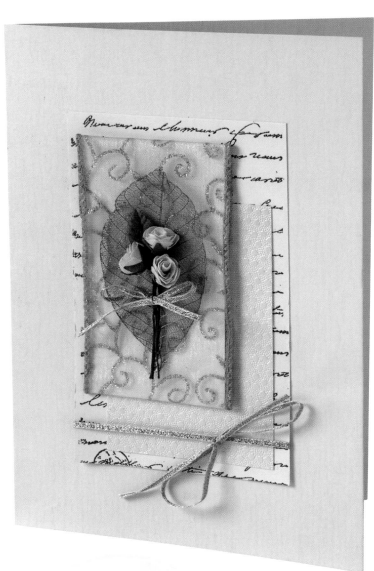

stamp smart

Paper roses and skeleton leaves give a lovely natural feel to this project. Handmade papers such as Mulberry paper would also work well here, particularly if torn with a soft feathered edge (see page 116).

Beaded Gems

The stamped flower on this card is treated with Glossy Accents, which gives a lovely glazed finish. The floral theme is picked up by the buttons and shaped gemstones, some of which are attached on to the inside of the card beneath the apertures.

1 Use the black ink pad stamp the image on to the larger piece of white card. Colour with the paints and use the Glossy Accents to cover the image. Allow to dry completely.

2 Fold the lilac card in half to make the base card. Punch or cut five squares across the bottom and down the right-hand side of the front of the base card, as shown.

3 Glue the pink card on to the back of the centre bottom aperture and the silver card through the top right aperture on to the inside of the base card. Glue the small square of white card in the bottom corner on the inside of the base card. Use glue dots to attach the buttons and flower shaped gems, as shown.

4 Wrap the ribbon around the left-hand side of the stamped flower image so that the image shows through it, and secure it at the back. Glue the image on to the gingham paper and then glue on to the front of the base card.

stamp smart
Other 3D embellishments such as shells, or pressed flowers could also be used to decorate the card, depending on the theme of the stamp used. Consider using recycled items such as spare buttons cut from old items of clothing.

YOU WILL NEED
Magenta '29107.R' stamp • StazOn® black ink pad • Lilac pearlescent card 14.5 x 29cm (5¾ x 11⅜in) for the base card • Pink gingham patterned paper 7cm (2¾in) square • Two pieces of white card, one 5.5 x 5cm (2⅛ x 2in), and one 1.5cm (½in) square • Pink card 3.5cm (1⅜in) square • Silver card 2.5cm (1in) square • Papermania buttons and shaped gemstones • Narrow sheer lilac ribbon 10cm (4in) in length • Watercolour paints in purple, pink and green • Glossy Accents • 2.5cm (1in) square punch (optional) • 3D foam pads • Glue dots • Glue stick

FINISHED SIZE 14.5cm (5¾in) square

Contemporary Christmas

Silver embossing powder is used here on glossy silver card to create this modern-styled Christmas card. Adhesive gems of differing sizes are applied then the edge of the card is cut using a border punch that embosses as it punches.

YOU WILL NEED

Elusive Images 'Christmas' stamps and clear acrylic mounting block • VersaMark™ ink pad • Brilliance 'Platinum Planet' pigment ink pad • Silver embossing powder • Two pieces of white card, one 15 x 20cm (5⅞ x 7⅞in) for the base card, and one 14.5 x 3cm (5¾ x 1⅛in) • Three pieces of silver card 4cm (1½in) square • Lilac shimmer ribbon 30cm (12in) in length • Papermania Adhesive Gemstones • Fiskars Border punch • Pink and lilac acrylic paint dabbers • 3D foam pads • Glue stick

FINISHED SIZE 15 x 10cm (5⅞ x 4in)

1 Use the VersaMark™ ink pad to stamp the images on to the three pieces of silver card.

2 Use the silver embossing powder to heat emboss the images. Stick the gemstones on to the images as shown.

3 Fold the large piece of white card in half to make the base card. Use the paint dabbers to colour the front half of the card. Colour the strip of white card in the same way.

4 Use the border punch to cut the front of the card about 2.5cm (1in) in from the right-hand edge. Tie ribbon around the front to conceal where the paint ends. Glue the strip of painted white card on to the inside right of the base card.

5 Use 3D foam pads to stick the silver squares on to the front of the base card at different angles to finish.

BEADED TREE

This simple triangle-shaped tag is stamped and heat embossed with silver embossing powder and then beads are threaded on to nylon fishing wire before being wrapped around the tag. The silver card is duller than the powder giving a slightly different finish to the glossy silver card used in the main project. *Stamp used: Hero Arts® 'Tiny Snowflake'.*

Terrific Tags and Pockets

Adding tags to a project is an instant way to create an unusual 3D effect, while pockets and envelopes make things interactive, requiring action to reveal what is inside – whether it is a gift or just a hidden message. A wide variety of tags and envelopes can be made from ready-made templates, or even from die cutting machines and punches. Many scrapbook paper manufacturers also provide purpose-made embellishments featuring tags and mini envelopes to co-ordinate with their paper ranges and ribbons.

Special Stationery

This simple folder has a large pocket in to which envelopes and notepaper can be placed. Pretty dragonflies and shimmering colours are accentuated with Glossy Accents and matching ribbon.

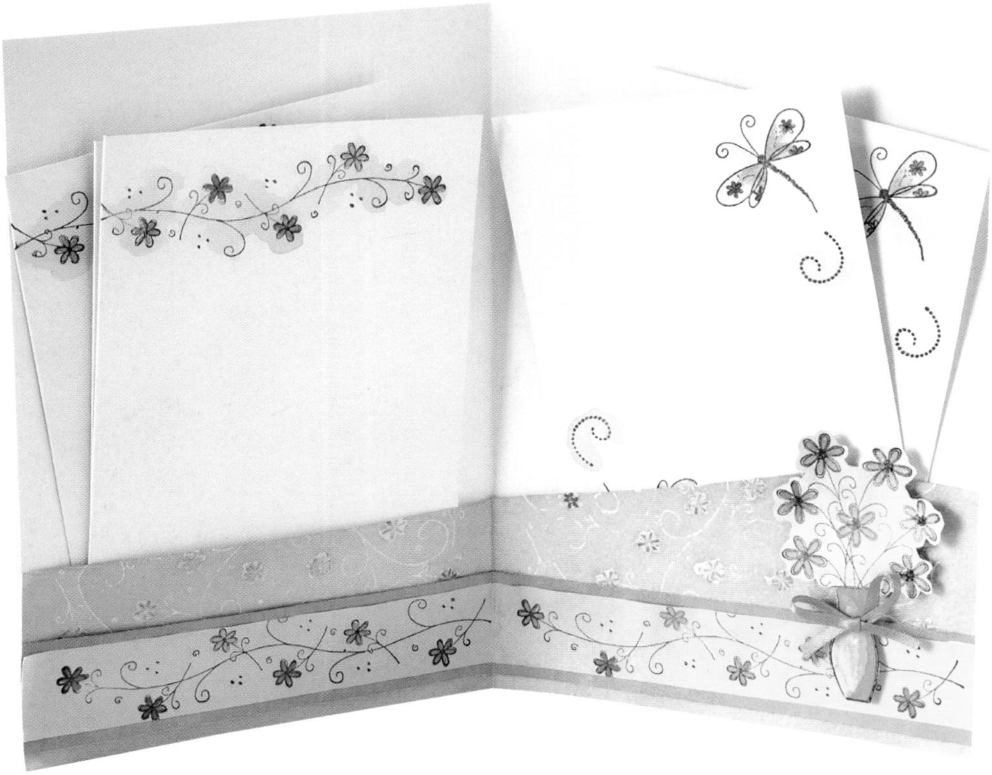

YOU WILL NEED

Aspects of Design 'Daisy Dreams' stamp sheet and clear acrylic mounting block ● StazOn® black ink pad ● VersaMark™ ink pad ● White embossing powder ● Eight pieces of white card, one A4 size (29.7 x 21cm / 11⅝ x 8¼in) for the folder, two 9 x 6cm (3½ x 2⅜in), one 10 x 7cm (4 x 2¾in), one 13.5 x 9.5cm (5⅜ x 3¾in), one 2.5 x 21cm (1 x 8¼in), one 3 x 21cm (1⅛ x 8¼in), and one 8 x 21cm (3⅛ x 8¼in) ● Starburst Stains 'Mermaid Seashells' ● Glossy Accents ● Watercolour paints in pink, red and yellow ● Narrow orange ribbon 10cm (4in) in length ● Plain envelopes and note cards ● 3D foam pads ● Glue stick

FINISHED SIZE 21 x 14.5cm (8¼ x 5¾in)

1 Use the VersaMark™ ink pad to stamp the floral background stamp on to the 8 x 21cm (3⅛ x 8¼in) and 13.5cm x 9.5cm (5⅜ x 3¾in) pieces of white card. Use the white embossing powder to heat emboss the images. Colour with the paints and then apply blobs of Glossy Accents over the top of the flowers. Leave to dry.

2 Once dry, brush the Sea Mint Green stain over the top of both pieces. Apply a second coat and leave to dry again. Apply a thin coat of Glory of the Seas Gold stain over the top. Take the 3 x 21cm (1⅛ x 8¼in) and 10 x 7cm (4 x 2¾in) pieces of white card and apply several coats of Cocklebells Coral stain. Leave to dry.

3 On to the 2.5 x 21cm (1 x 8¼in) strip apply one wash of Cocklebells Coral stain and allow to dry before stamping the border using the black ink pad. Colour the flowers with the paints.

4 On to the two pieces of 9 x 6cm (3½ x 2⅜in) card apply one wash of Cocklebells Coral stain and allow to dry before stamping the vase of flowers on to each piece using the black ink pad. Colour with the paints. Cut out one of the vases of flowers carefully around the outline.

5 Fold the large piece of white card in half to make the folder. Layer the vase of flowers on to the coral-coloured card and again on to the green stamped card. Glue on to the front of the folder adding a ribbon bow to the vase.

6 Take the strip of green-coloured card and draw a diagonal line 6cm (2⅜in) up from the bottom left-hand side and 8cm (3⅛in) up and 4cm (1½in) in from the right-hand side, then cut along the line. Glue the strip along the bottom, left and right sides only to make a pocket. Layer the other strips of card on to each other and glue on to the pocket.

7 Stick the cut out vase on to the right-hand side of the pocket using 3D foam pads and glue a ribbon bow on to the vase.

8 Decorate the envelopes and note cards by stamping the images with the black ink pad and carefully painting them. Add a thin wash of Glory of the Seas Gold stain around the stamped images.

stamp smart
Paint lots of sheets of paper with Starburst Stains in advance, so that you have a supply of dry paper to hand before starting a project. Save any off-cuts of the painted paper as they can be used in other craft projects.

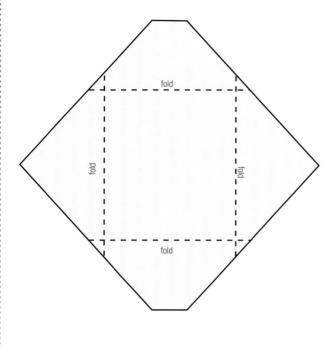

MAKING AN ENVELOPE

Cards are often made to fit standard shop-bought envelopes; however envelopes can be made to fit any card size. Templates are available in different shapes and sizes, but to make your own envelope simply add around 1cm (⅜in) to the height and 2cm (¾in) to the width of the card and make the base this size. Add a bottom and top flap, which should measure at least half of the height of the card, at the centre highest point. The side flaps are made by joining up the diagonals so that the whole shape makes a rectangle. Before folding in the side flaps cut 0.5cm (¼in) from each side of the top and bottom flap. Fold the side flaps inwards so that the creases align with the top and bottom flaps. Apply glue to the sides of the bottom flap and fold it over the side flaps. The top flap can be glued in the same way after the card is placed inside the envelope. A good tip is to carefully open out a shop-bought envelope. Use this to trace around on to stiff card, then trim to shape and use it as a template. Line envelopes with matching papers leftover from making the card. Cut the liner the same shape as the base of the envelope plus the top flap, but make it slightly smaller, and use glue to stick it inside the envelope.

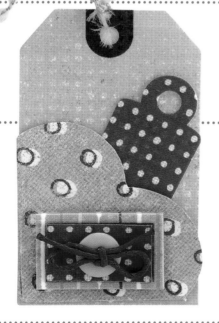

MAKING A TAG

Cut a rectangle shape from card. With the short edges at the top and bottom, start at the top left corner and measure and mark an equal distance down the left side and across the top of the shape. Join the points to make a diagonal line and cut across. Repeat from the top right corner on the right side to complete the tag shape. Punch a hole in the top using a small hole punch, and add a ribbon or other embellishments to finish.

Golden Glow

This tag-shaped book is decorated in soft apricots and gold paisley stamped images. A mini tag completes the design. Use the book as a mini photo album, changing the colours to match the theme.

YOU WILL NEED

Elusive Images 'UA4GW0157' stamp sheet and clear acrylic mounting block • Brilliance 'Galaxy Gold' pigment ink pad • VersaMark™ ink pad • Gold embossing powder • Two pieces of white card, one 4 x 7cm (1½ x 2¾in), and one 7 x 6cm (2¾ x 2⅜in) • Two pieces of gold card, one 3cm (1⅛in) square, and one 6.5 x 5cm (2½ x 2in) • Torn strip of gold vellum 4 x 6cm (1½ x 2⅜in) • Woodware tag book • Gold brad • Gold ribbon 20cm (8in) in length • Peach acrylic paint dabber • Glue stick

FINISHED SIZE 12.5 x 7.5cm (5 x 3in)

1 Paint the front of the tag book with the paint dabber, using a gentle swirling motion. Paint the two pieces of white card the same way. Build up the colour on the larger piece.

2 Use the gold ink to stamp the paisley image randomly over the front of the tag book.

3 Stamp the script image using the gold ink pad on to the smaller piece of painted card. Cut into a mini tag shape.

4 Wrap the strip of torn vellum around the mini tag and secure at the back with glue.

5 Layer on to the gold card and then on to the deeper painted white card and secure with the gold brad. Glue on to the front of the tag book.

6 Using the VersaMark™ ink pad and gold embossing powder, stamp and heat emboss the square patterned stamp on to the small square of gold card. Glue on to the mini tag.

7 Tie the ribbon through the tag book and secure with a bow.

TOOL KIT

To make this striking card, the stamped and heat-embossed images are chalked over, as are the edges of the tag-shaped card. A mini tag is placed inside the simple pocket. Wire and a Making Memories® charm co-ordinate with the tool theme and The English Paper Company scrapbook paper. *Stamps used: Stamps Away 'Tool Time'.*

Vouch Safe

This fresh and modern-styled mini wallet is ideal for holding gift vouchers, tokens or cash notes. The embellishments are all stamped including the buttons, ribbon and stitching.

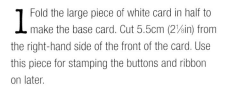

stamp smart

The buttons look even more realistic if tiny holes are punched through them using an eyelet setter.

1 Fold the large piece of white card in half to make the base card. Cut 5.5cm (2⅛in) from the right-hand side of the front of the card. Use this piece for stamping the buttons and ribbon on later.

2 Stamp the Layering Circles image randomly in various colours over the left-hand front of the base card. Use the Lime ink pad to stamp the stitched ribbon image down the inside right-hand side of the base card.

3 Stick the strip of white card on to the inside of the base card to make a pocket, by applying glue to the left and bottom edges only.

4 Fold the acetate in half and place over the white card. Apply a strip of glue on the back of the base card close to the fold and stick the acetate to this.

5 Punch a tag shape from the orange card. Glue on to the acetate so that it lies partly over the stamped area of the white card.

6 Stamp the buttons and ribbon images on to the leftover piece of white card using the coloured inks. Trim around the edges and stick on to the small pieces of coloured card as shown using 3D foam pads before gluing on to the front of the wallet. Cut the ribbon in half, place the two halves on top of each other so that they look as though they have been folded and staple them together. Cut the ends of the stamped ribbon in to points and glue on to the tag.

YOU WILL NEED

Hero Arts® 'Buttons Galore', 'Ribbons' and 'Layering Circles' stamps • ColorBox® 'Lime', 'Orange', 'Scarlet', 'Canary' and 'Orchid' pigment ink pads • Two pieces of white card, one 14.5 x 21cm (5¾ x 8¼in) for the base card, and one 5 x 10.5cm (2 x 4⅛in) • Orange card 8 x 5cm (3⅛ x 2in) • Pink card 4cm (1½in) square • Two pieces of lime-green card, one 4 x 2.5cm (½ x 1in), and one 2cm (¾in) square • Woodware large tag-shaped punch • Acetate 14.5 x 21cm (5¾ x 8¼in) • Stapler and staples • 3D foam pads • Glue stick

FINISHED SIZE 14.5 x 10.5cm (5¾ x 4⅛in)

Happy Holidays

This brightly coloured folksy card is embellished with a mini envelope, rub-on images and Glossy Accents, which really make it stand out. The style of the stamps give it a charming, hand-drawn appeal.

YOU WILL NEED

Doodlebug 'Home for the Holidays' stamp sheet and clear acrylic mounting block • VersaMark™ ink pad • Black embossing powder • Three pieces of white card, one 15 x 21cm (5⅞ x 8¼in) for the base card, one 6 x 4.5cm (2⅜ x 1¾in), and one 4 x 5cm (1½ x 2in) • Doodlebug paper 'Christmas Magic' 15 x 4cm (5⅞ x 1½in), 'Limeade Velvet' 11cm (4⅜in) square, 'Candy Cane Stripe' 8.5 x 7cm (3⅜ x 2¾in), 'Holly Jolly' 1.5 x 10.5cm (½ x 4⅛in) • Doodlebug 'Jolly Holly Days' Rub-Ons • Watercolour paints in red and green • Glossy Accents • Dovecraft Mini Envelopes Template • Glue stick

FINISHED SIZE 15 x 10.5cm (5⅞ x 4⅛in)

NEW HOME

These punched tags are threaded on to ribbon and mini pegs are used to hold them in place. The key charm also adds an extra tactile element to the design. The stamped images are coloured in the same shades as the Papermania scrapbook paper used. *Stamps used: Woodware 'On The Move' sheet.*

1 Fold the large piece of white card in half to make the base card. Glue the strip of Christmas Magic paper down the left-hand side. Glue the Candy Cane Stripe paper centrally on top.

2 Use the Limeade Velvet paper and template to cut the envelope, assemble and stick the flap down. Glue the envelope on to the Candy Cane Stripe paper. Glue the strip of Holly Jolly paper across the envelope.

3 Use the VersaMark™ ink pad to stamp the house on to the 6 x 4.5cm (2⅜ x 1¾in) piece of white card.

4 Use the black embossing powder to heat emboss the image. Repeat with the bauble image on to the 4 x 5cm (1½ x 2in) piece of white card, and the trees on to the bottom of the base card.

5 Colour the stamped images with watercolour paints and apply Glossy Accents. Place the stamped house inside the envelope. Use 3D foam pads to attach the bauble to the strip of Holly Jolly paper.

6 Place the Rub-Ons on to the card and burnish with the stick provided, following the manufacturer's guidance.

Collage-Style Creations

Stamping 'collage-style' is simply the act of adding lots of different images and embellishments within a theme. The theme can be whatever you want, as long as you can find the stamps and 3D trimmings to match. The collage images can be made from lots of different stamps or from single stamps that contain multiple images, so the effect can be duplicated very simply using just one stamp. Torn scraps of paper and ageing techniques such as the application of ink or chalk to edges can also give an heirloom quality to a collage-style project.

Baby Shower

This pretty tin can be used to display gifts for a new baby and is a keepsake in itself. The images are stamped and heat embossed using white embossing powder, which co-ordinates with the patterned paper used. Shaped buttons and pretty ribbon also add to the collage effect.

YOU WILL NEED

Woodware 'Baby Zone FRCL057' stamp sheet and clear acrylic mounting block • VersaMark™ ink pad • White embossing powder • White card 15 x 10cm (5⅞ x 4in) • Sandylion scrapbook paper 'Expecting Flowers' 6.5 x 12cm (2½ x 4¾in) and 'Shower Stripes' 9cm (3½in) square • Anna Griffin 'AG1129' paper 8 x 6cm (3⅛ x 2⅜in) • Papermania punched paper hearts and buttons • Sen Plus napkin pins • Two pieces of yellow gingham ribbon 15cm (5⅞in) in length • Pail 12.5cm (5in) high x 11cm (4⅜in) diameter • Paints or coloured pencils in pink, green, blue and yellow • Glue dots • Glue stick

FINISHED SIZE 12.5cm (5in) high x 11cm (4⅜in) diameter

1 Arrange the stamps on to the acrylic block close to each other. Use the VersaMark™ ink pad to carefully ink the stamps, ensuring that the rubber is evenly coated. Stamp the images on to the white card.

2 Sprinkle white embossing powder over the stamped images and tap off the excess powder, returning it to the container. Remove stray powder with a paint brush. Heat with the heat gun until the powder melts.

3 Trim around the edges of the images carefully following the outlines. Colour the images with the paints or pencils.

4 Glue the strip of Expecting Flowers paper around the pail. Cut a 7cm (2¾in) circle from the Shower Stripes paper and stick on to the lid.

5 Tie the lengths of gingham ribbon around the handles in to bows.

6 Make a tag shape from the Anna Griffin paper, and glue it on to the tin to conceal the join of the Expecting Flowers paper.

7 Glue the stamped images and hearts on to the pail as shown, adding the buttons with glue dots to finish.

stamp smart
The same basic idea can be adapted for other occasions, such as a bridal shower. The pail could also be decorated and used for storing everyday household items, such as stationery.

Cute Clipboard

This project is great for using up leftover scraps of paper from other projects. Here, a simple colour scheme and subtle inks create a harmonious, pretty theme. Adding a paper flower and co-ordinating ribbon further enhances the collage effect. Only one stamp has been used, but a similar result can be achieved using a number of different stamps of a similar theme and printing the images randomly over the surface of the paper.

1 Using the distress ink pads, stamp the image once on to each of the scrapbook papers. Stamping close to the edge will make less waste.

2 Using the Lullaby Check paper as the base, tear strips of the other stamped pieces and glue them directly over the top of the base layer, aligning the stamped images.

3 Attach the paper blossom to the image using the brad provided. Trim the whole lot to size and glue it to the front cover of the notebook.

4 Cover the clipboard with the large piece of Anna Griffin paper trimmed to size, and secure with glue. Tie lengths of the ribbon through the top of the clip.

5 Cover the top edge of the clothes peg with a leftover piece of the stamped paper. Cover the pencil by wrapping a cut-off strip of the same paper around it and securing with glue. Glue the peg on to the clipboard and clamp the pencil in it.

6 Use the stapler to make a loop from the ribbon. Slide the loop around the top of the pencil and glue the loop to the clipboard. Glue the notebook on to the front of the clipboard to finish.

stamp smart
Instead of covering the clipboard with scrapbook paper, try painting a base coat using acrylic paint. The board can then also be stamped and decorated in a similar way to the notebook.

YOU WILL NEED
Stamps Happen Inc 'Vintage Bulb Collage #90338' • Ranger 'Worn Lipstick' and 'Weathered Wood' distress ink pads • Daisy D's scrapbook paper 'Lullaby Check – Nursery' and 'Polka Dot – Nursery Pink', one piece of each 17cm x 12cm (6⅝ x 4¾in) • Two pieces of Anna Griffin 'AG1129' scrapbook paper, one 25 x 17cm (9⅞ x 6⅝in) to cover the clipboard, and one 17cm x 12cm (6⅝ x 4¾in) • Making Memories® 'Wildflower Spotlight' paper blossom • Notebook 14cm x 10cm (5½ x 4in) • Clipboard 23 x 15cm (9 x 5⅞in) • Maya Road 'Laughter' ribbons pack • Clothes peg • Pencil • Stapler and staples • Glue stick

FINISHED SIZE 23 x 15cm (9 x 5⅞in)

Magnolia Memories

Stampbord™ has a fine clay-like surface that when scratched with a needle produces striations. The technique is used here to highlight areas of the stamped image and works particularly well with etched-style stamps where the striations should follow the stamped lines. The direct application of ink straight from the pad on to the card produces a lovely soft background. The same ink is used to stamp the images, creating a subtle yet effective result.

1 Fold the large piece of white card in half to make the base card. Use the chalk ink pads to colour the front of the card by rubbing directly on to the paper (see page 113). Allow to dry.

2 Using the same ink pads, stamp the butterfly image randomly spaced over the front of the base card.

3 Using the same 'direct to paper' technique and inks as in step 1, colour the other piece of white card. Once dry, cut a piece from the card to measure 8.5cm (3⅜in) square and using the black ink stamp the Manuscript Background image over the top and allow to dry. Cut the leftover piece of white card to measure 6cm (2⅜in) square and put to one side for later.

4 Use the chalk ink pads to gently colour the Stampbord™ tile and allow it to dry. Use the black ink pad to stamp the Magnolia image on to the tile. Once dry, use a needle or similar sharp tool to scratch the surface of the tile to reveal the clay beneath, making textural highlights.

5 Layer the Stampbord™ tile on top of smallest square of black card. Layer again on to the coloured piece of white card that was put aside in step 3. Layer on to the middle-sized square of black card before gluing on to the Manuscript stamped card. Layer on to the largest square of black card before finally gluing all the layers to the front of the base card to finish.

stamp smart

To achieve a glossy finish, place the stamped tile face down on to an embossing ink pad and sprinkle with clear embossing powder before heat setting. Repeat three times for a smooth topcoat – any less than this and the surface might appear pitted.

YOU WILL NEED

Hero Arts® 'Manuscript Background H2141' stamp • Rubbadubbadoo 'Springtime SNS-ST' stamp set and 'Butterfly' stamp • ColorBox® 'Rose Coral', 'Peach Pastel' and 'Yellow Citrus' chalk ink pads • StazOn® black ink pad • Two pieces of white card, one 13 x 26cm (5⅛ x 10¼in) for the base card, and one at least 9 x 16cm (3½ x 6¼in) • Three pieces of black card, one 5.5cm (2⅛in) square, one 7cm (2¾in) square and one 9.5cm (3¾in) • Stampbord™ tile 5cm (2in) square • Needle (or similar sharp tool) • Glue stick

FINISHED SIZE 13cm (5⅛in) square

Elegant Journal

A shop-bought notebook has been decorated using a simple colour scheme that co-ordinates with the front cover. Over stamping the image a second time and adding torn edges are both quick yet effective techniques. The background could be made using different themed images, however here the simplicity of the script stamp works well with the flower shape, and a ribbon adds the finishing touch.

1 Using the flower stamp and the Cyan and Seaglass ink pads, stamp the image on to the strip of white card. Over stamp the image again using a touch of brown ink.

2 Tie a knot in the piece of ribbon and glue it on to the card towards the bottom of the flower.

3 Tear the sides of the turquoise card to reveal the chamfered edge (see page 116). Glue the stamped flower and ribbon on top of this.

4 Using the Manuscript Background stamp and the brown ink pad, stamp the image twice on to the larger piece of white card. Apply the Seaglass ink around all four edges of the card.

5 Glue the mounted flower image on to the Manuscript Background image and layer on to the brown card. Glue on to the front of the notebook to complete the journal.

stamp smart

Using clear stamps and acrylic blocks ensures that you can stamp the image a second time on top of the first image with perfect accuracy.

YOU WILL NEED

Stampendous 'Pressed Flowers SSC024' clear stamps • Hero Arts® 'Manuscript Background H2141' stamp • StazOn® 'Timber Brown' ink pad • ColorBox® 'Cyan' and 'Seaglass' pigment ink pads • Strip of white card 14.5 x 2.5cm (5¾ x 1in) • Turquoise card 14.5 x 8cm (5¾ x 3⅛in) • White card 14.5 x 10.5cm (5¾ x 4⅛in) • Brown card 15 x 11cm (5⅞ x 4⅜in) • Turquoise journal or notebook 21 x 15cm (8¼ x 5⅞in) • Turquoise and white striped ribbon 12cm (5in) in length • Glue stick

FINISHED SIZE 21 x 15cm (8¼ x 5⅞in)

Butterfly and Buttons

Simple 3D découpage is used here in combination with collage-style elements for a fantastic result. The main image is produced using just one stamp, and torn coloured paper is added prior to stamping the image to add to the collage effect. The wings of the butterfly are bent upwards giving the feeling of movement. This card looks complex but is actually very easy to make.

YOU WILL NEED

Inkadinkado Stamps 'Tin Can Mail 91619.X'
● Hero Arts® 'Long Writing Background F2674'
stamp ● ColorBox® 'Lavender', 'Robin's Egg' and
'Chestnut' pigment ink pads ● Brilliance 'Galaxy
Gold' pigment ink pad ● Turquoise card 22 x 15cm
(8⅝ x 5⅞in) for the base card ● Three pieces of
white card, two 9 x 10.5cm (3½ x 4⅛in), one 10
x 11.5cm (4 x 4½in) ● Small scrap of coloured
paper ● Blue and white gingham ribbon 14cm
(5½in) in length ● Three blue buttons ● Glue stick

FINISHED SIZE 11 x 15cm (4⅜ x 5⅞in)

1 Using the Lavender and Robin's Egg ink pads carefully sponge areas of one of the smaller pieces of white card with the ink. Glue a small scrap of coloured paper on to the top of the card.

2 Use the Chestnut ink pad to stamp the image on to the card. Rub the gold ink pad on to the edges of the card and allow it to dry. Glue this centrally on top of the larger piece of white card.

3 Use the Lavender and Robin's Egg ink pads to stamp the image on to the remaining small piece of white card. Cut out the butterfly and bend the wings upwards. Glue the body part of the butterfly directly over the top of the first image.

4 Fold the turquoise card in half to make a base card. Using the Long Writing Background stamp and gold ink, stamp the image on the left-hand side of the front of the base card. Glue the ribbon along the left-hand side, securing the top edge on the back of the card and the bottom edge inside it.

5 Glue the buttons on to the ribbon so that they are equally spaced and central. Glue the mounted stamped panel on to the base card to finish.

SIMPLE COLLAGE

To achieve a simple collage-style effect without too much effort, glue scraps of leftover paper on to a base of white card. Once dry, stamp a single image using a collage-style stamp and solvent ink – this will ensure the image will dry on coated paper. Layer on to coloured card and glue on a ribbon bow to finish. *Stamp used: Hampton Arts 'Clear Expressions C84267'.*

Nature's Ways

Here, the same image is stamped twice and layered on to darker card. A skeleton leaf, button and ribbon complement the collage style. Soft coloured pencils are used to colour the stamped design and are chosen to co-ordinate with the shadow inks and scrapbook paper used to cover the front of the card. The project can be left as a card or the front part can be used to cover a notebook to make a nature journal. Other natural embellishments, such as twigs or seed heads, could be used to enhance the collage.

1 Fold the large piece of white card in half to make the base card and cover the front with the scrapbook paper.

2 Using the shadow ink pads and shadow block, stamp the image several times on to the two remaining pieces of white card. Using the Nature Journal stamp and the brown ink pad, stamp the image on to each piece of white card.

3 Layer one piece of the stamped white card on to the larger piece of brown card before gluing centrally on to the front of the base card.

4 Cut out the second stamped image around the edge of the wooden frame section and layer on to the smaller piece of brown card. Punch two holes at the bottom and thread the ribbon through, tying it in a knot at the front. Glue the whole lot centrally on to the base card.

5 Colour parts of the image with the coloured pencils. Cut four corners from the scrapbook paper cut-offs and glue on to the inner stamped image. Use a brown coloured pencil to draw a dashed line across each corner.

6 Glue the skeleton leaf and button on to the centre panel as shown to finish.

YOU WILL NEED

Stamps Happen Inc 'Nature Journal #90282' • Hero Arts® 'Three Irregular Blocks G2622' stamp • Hero Arts® 'Vanilla', 'Rose' and 'Leaf' shadow ink pads • StazOn® 'Timber Brown' ink pad • Three pieces of white card, one 17 x 26cm (6⅝ x 10¼in) for the base card, and two 13 x 9cm (5⅛ x 3½in) • Two pieces of brown card, one 10 x 7cm (4 x 2¾in), and one 13.5 x 10cm (5⅜ x 4in) • Kelly Panacci scrapbook paper 17 x 13cm (6⅝ x 5⅛in) plus cut-offs • Papermania 'PMA7501' ribbon 18cm (7in) in length • Coloured pencils in similar shades to the shadow ink pads • Hole punch • Small button • Skeleton leaf • Glue stick

FINISHED SIZE 17 x 13cm (6⅝ x 5⅛in)

Bon Voyage

This large card is decorated with travel-themed images. It contains a pocket so can be used to store mementoes of a trip such as train and air tickets, postcards or photographs.

YOU WILL NEED

Inkadinkado Stamps 'Tin Can Mail 91667.Y', '1233.J', and '92715.0' • ColorBox® 'Chestnut' and 'Burnt Sienna' chalk ink pads • Papermania 'Classic Embellishment Kit' • Two pieces of white card, one 21 x 29.5cm (8¼ x 11⅝in) for the base card, and one 9 x 13cm (3½ x 5⅛in) • Lemon and blue chalk and cotton wool ball • Brown ribbon 20cm (8in) in length • Making Memories® Pewter Photo Anchors • Glue stick

FINISHED SIZE 21 x 15cm (8¼ x 5⅞in)

1 Fold the large piece of white card 7cm (2¾in) from the left and right edge, to make a zigzag or concertina card. Cover the front panel with the patterned cream paper, and the inside with the brown text paper.

2 Cut an 8 x 15cm (3⅛ x 5⅞in) strip from the diamond patterned paper and glue the bottom, left and right edges to the inside of the card to make a pocket.

3 Use the inks to stamp the images of the camera and map on to the white card, apply chalks to the surface with the cotton wool ball to add colour (see page 114).

4 Stamp the compass on to patterned paper and glue all the images on to the inside of the card, tucking them into the pocket slightly.

5 Add the Photo Anchors and other embellishments as shown. To finish, thread the ribbon through the card buckle and glue on to the pocket.

SEA DREAMS

Actual shells are used to accentuate the collage-style of this stamp – but remember to use shells bought at a craft shop rather than taking them from the beach. The gold embossed image is painted using Starburst Stains 'Mermaid Seashells', the same paint is applied to paper and then crumpled to produce the background paper, which unifies the design. *Stamp used: Inkadinkado Stamps 'Tin Can Mail 91675.Y'*

Mix & Match Materials

Almost any surface can be stamped on as long as the right ink is used. The projects in this chapter are made by stamping on to polymer clay, shrink plastic, acetate, vellum, fabric and metal to create some highly imaginative and unusual 3D cards and gifts. Always read the instructions on ink pads carefully to see what materials they are suitable for, and then get stamping …

Welcome Baby

Polymer clay and even sealing waxes can be stamped on to produce imprints. In this project the stamped polymer clay produces an effect rather like a cast of a baby's handprints. A soft heat-embossed border complements the theme. Use shades of blue for a baby boy.

YOU WILL NEED

Inkadinkado Stamps 'It's A Baby' stamp sheet and clear acrylic mounting block • VersaMark™ ink pad • Pink embossing powder • White card 21 x 15cm (8¼ x 5⅞in) for the base card • Making Memories® 'Bella' paper pad • Making Memories® 'Bella' ribbon 12cm (5in) in length • Making Memories® buttons • White polymer clay • Wavy-edged scissors • Glue stick

FINISHED SIZE 10.5 x 15cm (4⅛ x 5⅞in)

1 Roll out the polymer clay until it is about 3mm (⅛in) thick. Press the handprints stamps (mounted together side by side on the acrylic block) firmly in to the surface of the clay.

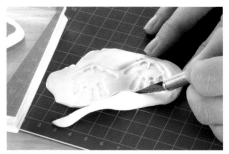

2 Cut around the edges of the clay and bake in an oven as directed.

3 Cut a 3.5cm (1⅜in) strip from the striped paper. Using the VersaMark™ ink pad and pink embossing powder, stamp and heat emboss the image repeatedly on the strip.

4 Fold the white card in half to make the base card and glue a 9 x 10.5cm (3½ x 4⅛in) piece of spotted paper on to the front right-hand side.

5 Glue the gingham paper on to the left-hand side. Glue the strip of stamped paper across the front.

6 Cut a 3cm (1⅛in) strip of yellow paper with the wavy-edged scissors and glue down the left-hand side. Glue the ribbon on top.

7 Glue the handprints on to a 3 x 6cm (1⅛ x 2⅜in) rectangle of the gingham paper and then on to yellow paper. Tear the bottom to reveal the chamfered edge (see page 116) and glue on to the base card.

8 Glue the buttons on to the front of the card as shown to finish.

stamp smart

When stamping on to clay you need to apply more pressure than you would to stamp on to paper. The more pressure applied, the deeper and more effective the cast will be.

Shrink plastic

Shrink plastic is a fun-to-use product that shrinks to about one-third of its size when heated. It can be used to make wonderfully unusual embellishments on cards or for quirky gifts.

- The plastic should be lightly sanded on one side before it is stamped with an image. If it is not pre-sanded, use a sanding block and sand in all directions to produce a cross-hatch pattern (**1**).

- Stamp images on to shrink plastic using a solvent ink pad or one recommended for most surfaces, such as StazOn® or Brilliance pigment ink pads.

- Colour the stamped image with chalks, ink or paint, but be aware that the colour intensifies during the heating process.

- Either use a heat gun or follow the manufacturer's instructions to heat the plastic until it shrinks to a flat tile much smaller than its original size. The plastic will curl and fold during the heating process – continue to heat until it becomes flat again (**2**). Use a cocktail stick to hold the plastic down while heating to help to minimize curling.

- While the plastic is still warm place it face down and press it using an acrylic or wooden stamping block to flatten it (**3**). Alternatively it can be shaped slightly with the fingers so that when it cools it will retain its new shape (**4**).

stamp smart
If your final object requires any holes in it, make them prior to shrinking the plastic, as it is much easier than trying to do it afterwards.

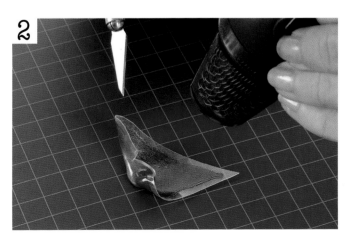

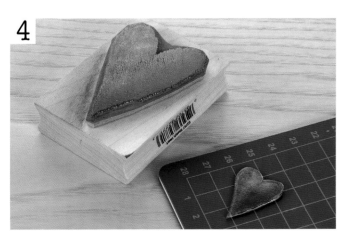

Pretty Hydrangeas

The tiny bees on this card are made using shrink plastic. Stamping the bees on to ordinary card would produce images too large for the scale of the flowers and so clear shrink plastic has been used instead, which also helps suggest the transparency of their wings.

SHRINKING GIFTS

Shrink plastic is used here to make a key ring and luggage tag – it can also be used to make jewellery items. Remember to punch the holes prior to shrinking. *Stamps used: Aspects of Design 'Daisy Dreams' sheet and Paper Nation 'Fisherman'.*

YOU WILL NEED

Rubbadubbadoo 'Hydrangea', 'Butterfly' and 'Bee' stamps • StazOn® black ink pad • VersaMark™ ink pad • Heat It Up black sparkle embossing powder • Three pieces of clear shrink plastic 7cm (2¾in) square • Sandylion 'RMSCB78' scrapbook paper 13cm (5⅛in) square • Two pieces of white card, one 13 x 26cm (5⅛ x 10¼in) for the base card, and one 13cm (5⅛in) square • Brush markers in purple, yellow and green • Lilac ribbon 40cm (16in) in length • Glitter glue • 3D foam pads • Glue stick

FINISHED SIZE 13cm (5⅛in) square

1 Use the VersaMark™ ink pad to stamp the hydrangea image on to the smaller piece of white card.

2 Use the black sparkle embossing powder to heat emboss the image. Repeat to make a second image. Cut around the outlines carefully to avoid chipping the powder. Repeat the process with the butterfly stamp.

3 Use the brush markers to colour the images, blending the colours with a paintbrush and a little water.

4 Use the black ink pad to stamp the bee image on to each piece of shrink plastic. Colour with the brush markers and carefully cut around the outlines before heating.

5 Fold the large piece of white card in half to make the base card. Glue the hydrangea images on to the front and carefully cut around the edges following the outline on the right-hand side only. Stick the piece of patterned paper on to the inside of the card and tie the ribbon around the front left-hand side.

6 Attach the stamped butterfly using 3D foam pads, and glue the bees on to the base card as shown.

7 Highlight areas with the glitter glue and allow to dry flat.

Acetate

Acetate is thin transparent plastic that usually comes in sheets. Some types are heat resistant so that embossing powder can be used on them. Permanent solvent-type inks are needed when stamping on acetate. The reverse of the stamped image can be coloured with glitter and transparent glue to achieve a stained glass window effect. Acetate can also be coloured with pens, such as peel-off markers, overhead projector pens or Sakura gel pens.

Oriental Poppies

Metal leaf gives a luxurious quality to this pretty Chinese-themed card, applied to acetate simply using a double-sided sticky sheet. Stamping on to a second acetate sheet creates a layered effect. Glitter adds an extra touch of sparkle.

1 Use the VersaMark™ ink pad to stamp the image centrally on to one of the pieces of acetate.

2 Use the black embossing powder to heat emboss the image.

3 Place the acetate face down and apply the Art Glitter Adhesive on to the poppy using the fine-tip applicator, carefully staying with the outline. Sprinkle the red glitter over the top, return the excess glitter to the container and allow to dry completely.

4 Take the second piece of acetate and remove the backing from the punch tape and place centrally on to the top. Remove the top piece of backing and sprinkle the Metal Leaf over the top until the whole area is covered. With a large paintbrush gently rub to remove the excess and return the unused pieces to the pack.

5 Place the two layers of acetate face up on top of each other and secure a brad through each corner.

6 Fold the red card in half to make the base card and stick the layers of acetate on top using tiny blobs of glue underneath the leafed area.

YOU WILL NEED

Hampton Arts 'Asian Poppy' stamp • VersaMark™ ink pad • Black embossing powder • Two sheets of acetate 14.5 x 10.5cm (5¾ x 4⅛in) • Red card 14.5 x 21cm (5¾ x 8¼in) for the base card • Eberhard Faber Metal Leaf Flakes • Four black brads • Glue Dots double-sided punch tape • Ultra-fine red glitter • Art Glitter Adhesive and fine-tip applicator • Glue stick

FINISHED SIZE 14.5 x 10.5cm (5¾ x 4⅛in)

Parisian Chic

On this stylish card, the image is stamped on to the acetate and also on to the layer below. The two layers are aligned and Flower Soft™ is used to add a realistic 3D quality to the feather boa. Patterned scrapbook papers provide a pretty background.

YOU WILL NEED

Stamps Happen Inc 'Paris Socialite' • StazOn® black ink pad • Sandylion 'RMSCB316' paper 14.5 x 10cm (5¾ x 4in) • Acetate 14.5 x 10cm (5¾ x 4in) • Two pieces of white card, one 17.5 x 26cm (6⅞ x 10¼in) for the base card, and one 9 x 13cm (3½ x 5⅛in) • White glitter card 15.5 x 11cm (6 x 4⅜in) • Flower Soft™ • General-purpose tacky craft glue • Two silver brads • Watercolour paints in shades of pink • Glue stick

FINISHED SIZE 17.5 x 13cm (6⅞ x 5⅛in)

1 Use the black ink pad to stamp the image on to the smaller piece of white card.

2 Cut around the edges of the figure only and colour using the paints.

3 Stamp the image again centrally on to the acetate, then place the acetate over the patterned paper and secure a brad in the top and bottom corners of the left-hand side.

4 Glue the stamped figure directly underneath the acetate, aligning it carefully.

5 Fold the large piece of white card in half to make the base card. Glue the layered acetate on to the glitter card, and then on to the front of the base card.

6 Apply the craft glue to the acetate over the boa and cuffs. Sprinkle the Flower Soft™ over the top and allow to dry flat.

OTHER ACETATE TECHNIQUES

Acetate can be used in numerous different ways for stamping. Try smothering the reverse side with glue and then adding drops of ink. Place a layer of tissue paper over the top and allow to dry. Turn the acetate over and stamp on top to create a stamped image with a pretty background. Alternatively you can use acetate to create stained glass window effects over apertures, such as the card on page 43.

Vellum

Vellum is a translucent paper that looks very effective when stamped. It can usually be heat embossed and produces a lovely chamfered edge when torn (see page 116).

Wedding Wishes

This classic-styled card is made by stamping vellum with Brilliance ink to produce a subtle background paper. White foam is heated and the same stamp is pressed into the warm surface. Paper rosebuds, ribbon and ring charms complete the wedding theme.

1 Use the gold ink to stamp the image on to both pieces of vellum.

2 Layer the pieces of vellum on to the larger pieces of gold card and secure a brad in each corner.

3 Gently heat the foam with a heat gun until it becomes slightly soft, taking care not to burn the surface. Press the stamp firmly in to the heated foam and allow to cool before removing the stamp. Glue the foam centrally on to the largest piece of layered vellum.

4 Punch a heart from the remaining piece of gold card and glue the ring charms on top.

5 Bunch a few of the roses together and wrap one of the wire stems around the rest to make a bouquet. Glue on to the smaller piece of layered vellum.

6 Take the white card and make a fold 9.5cm (3¾in) from the left. Fold the right-hand side in to meet the left folded side. Stick the small piece of vellum and flowers on to the right-hand side.

7 Wrap the ribbon around the whole card from the left-hand side at the front around the back, and around to the right-hand side at the front and tie the ribbon with a bow just above the bouquet to secure it.

8 Glue the large piece of layered vellum on to the front of the base card over the top of the ribbon.

YOU WILL NEED

Aspects of Design 'Daisy Dreams' stamp sheet and clear acrylic mounting block • Brilliance 'Galaxy Gold' pigment ink pad • Two pieces of white vellum, one 9 x 8cm (3½ x 3⅛in), and one 9 x 3cm (3½ x 1⅛in) • White foam sheet 6 x 5cm (2⅜ x 2in) • Three pieces of gold card, one 10 x 9cm (4 x 3¾in), one 10 x 4cm (4 x 1½in), and one 6 x 5cm (2⅜ x 2in) • White stripe embossed card 11 x 29cm (4⅜ x 11⅜in) for the base card • Paper roses and leaves • White and gold ribbon 50cm (20in) in length • Large heart punch • Eight gold brads • Plastic ring charms • Glue stick

FINISHED SIZE 11 x 14.5cm (4⅜ x 5¾in)

Vellum Votives

These decorative candles are made from strips of vellum that are stamped and heat embossed using a mixture of different embossing powders. The vellum is torn to reveal a chamfered edge and beads are added to finish. The candles are for decoration only and should not be lit without removing the vellum first.

1 Use the VersaMark™ ink pad to stamp the image repeatedly on to the strips of vellum.

2 Sprinkle the gold embossing powder over the stamped image and tap off the excess powder returning it to the jar. Repeat with each embossing powder allowing the powder to cover different areas of the image. Remove stray powder with a paintbrush. Heat with the heat gun until the powder melts.

3 Tear the edges of the vellum so that a chamfered edge is made (see page 116).

4 Wrap the vellum around the candle and secure with double-sided tape.

5 Decorate the candle with beads by wrapping metallic thread around the candle, threading on the beads and securing with a knot to finish.

YOU WILL NEED

Elusive Images 'UA4GW0157' stamp sheet and clear acrylic mounting block • VersaMark™ ink pad
• Gold, Verdi Gris and Copper embossing powders
• Vellum cut into 7cm (2¾in) strips • Candles
• Beads • Metallic thread • Double-sided tape

FINISHED SIZE depends on candle size

stamp smart
Rubbing the reverse of the vellum with an embossing tool will give it a lovely frosted appearance.

Fabric

When stamping on to fabric, make sure you iron it first as any creases will affect the process. Experiment with different colours and types of fabric to produce varied results. The edges of the fabric can be frayed, but if you prefer neat edges use iron-on interfacing on the reverse of the image before the edges are cut.

Flowery Jotter

This cheerful notebook is made using the Zutter Bind-it-All system, but a ready-made notebook can be used instead. Dye ink pads are used to stamp the flower on to the cotton fabric. Use fine-tipped brush markers to pick out detail in the leaf veins once the image has been stamped. A peel-off flower border completes the look.

1 Assemble the cover and inner pages using the Zutter Bind-it-All system. Glue the large piece of foil paper on to the right-hand side of the cover.

2 Glue the strip of foil paper on to the left-hand side of the green card and glue this centrally on to the front of the notebook.

3 Colour in the outline stickers with the peel-off markers and remove from the sheet. Place on to the striped border.

4 Using the dye ink pads, stamp the image on to the fabric and allow to dry completely.

5 Back the fabric with the iron-on interfacing and neaten the edges.

6 Glue the fabric on to the green card on the front of the notebook to finish.

stamp smart
Because the fabric won't be washed dye ink can be used – you only need to use specialist fabric dye if an item needs to be washable.

YOU WILL NEED

Hero Arts® 'Jamaican forget-me-knot' stamp • ColorBox® 'Cranberry' and 'Green' dye ink pads • Pale green card 12cm (4¾in) square • Two pieces of Papermania double-sided foil paper, one 15 x 8cm (5⅞ x 3⅛in), and one 12 x 3cm (4¾ x 1⅛in) • Zutter Bind-it-All machine and 15.5cm (6in) covers (or suitable ready-made notebook) • Papermania outline stickers and peel-off markers • White or cream cotton fabric 10 x 7cm (4 x 2¾in) • Iron-on interfacing 10 x 7cm (4 x 2¾in) • Glue stick

FINISHED SIZE 15cm (5⅞in) square

Metal and Foil

Sheets of thin metal or foil can be stamped on using solvent-based ink. An embossing tool can be used to draw along the outline of the image to produce raised dry-embossed areas, which are wonderfully tactile.

Christmas Discs

CDs and DVDs of your home movies or photo slide shows always make great gifts, but can be personalized even further by stamping them. Here the theme is a child's nativity play, and the decorated disk is presented in a simple wallet, which includes its own gift card.

1 Use the black ink pad to stamp the nativity image on to the disk. Use the Soufflé pens to colour the image and allow it to dry completely.

2 Use the black ink pad to stamp the tree image on to both pieces of foil. Trim around the edge close to the outline. Use an embossing tool to trace over the outlines carefully. Use the pens to colour in one of the images. Apply the adhesive pearls to the baubles of both trees.

3 Fold the pearlescent card in half and cover the inside with the snowflake paper. Make a simple pocket from the striped paper by gluing it on to the bottom of the inside of the wallet on the bottom and side edges only.

4 Place the peel-off snowflakes on to the front of the card and the stickers on to the square piece of pale blue card.

5 Tear the edges of the strip of snowflake paper and stick across the pale blue square card. Stick the uncoloured tree on to the front and add peel-offs to each side before gluing centrally on to the front of the wallet.

6 Fold the remaining piece of blue card in half and decorate with stickers and torn snowflake paper. Glue the coloured tree on top.

7 Place the mini card into the left of the open wallet and the stamped DVD into the right.

YOU WILL NEED

Paper Nation 'Nativity Boys' stamps • Papermania 'PMA 10030' stamps • StazOn® black ink pad • Pearlescent blue card 13 x 26cm (5⅛ x 10¼in) for the wallet • Two pieces of pale blue card, one 10 x 15cm (4 x 5⅞in), and one 7cm (2¾in) square • Francis Meyer paper, three pieces of 'Let it Snow', one 13 x 26cm (5⅛ x 10¼in), one 7 x 1cm (2¾ x ⅜in), and one 5 x 7cm (2 x 2¾in), plus 'Snowy Stripes' 6 x 26cm (2⅜ x 10¼in) • Two pieces of silver foil 8 x 7cm (3⅛ x 2¾in) • Silver snowflake peel-off stickers • Snowflake stickers • Adhesive pearls • Sakura Soufflé pens • Glue stick

FINISHED SIZE 13cm (5⅛in) square

Perfect Paper Shaping

The art of paper shaping encompasses many different techniques to take you from a flat piece of paper to a 3D work of art. Methods include making gift boxes and bags, curling paper flower petals and leaves, knot-making and decorative folding techniques such as origami, teabag and iris folding. The projects in this chapter demonstrate a handful of simple skills to get you confidently paper shaping in next to no time.

Gorgeous Gift

This pretty box is made using lightweight card that has been stamped and heat embossed with white embossing powder. Coloured ink is then applied directly to the paper and the image appears almost ghost-like. A simple tag and large flower embellishment completes the project.

YOU WILL NEED

Anna Griffin 'With Gratitude' stamp set and clear acrylic mounting block ● VersaMark™ ink pad ● White embossing powder ● Brilliance 'Pearlescent Orchid' pigment ink pad ● Lightweight white card A4 size (29.7 x 21cm / 11⅝ x 8¼in) ● Two pieces of white card, one 2 x 4cm (¾ x 1½in) and one 3 x 5cm (1⅛ x 2in) ● Making Memories® 'Jumbo Blossom Wildflower Cream' ● Double-sided tape

FINISHED SIZE 7 x 7 x 5cm (2¾ x 2¾ x 2in)

1 Enlarge the template on page 119 by 50% on a photocopier, then use it to trace and cut out the box shape from the lightweight card.

2 Use the VersaMark™ ink pad to stamp the image all over the shape. Use the white embossing powder to heat emboss the image.

3 Rub the Pearlescent Orchid ink pad over the top of the stamped card and gently rub off the excess with a tissue or cloth.

4 Fold the card along the score lines and stick the flaps together with double-sided tape.

5 Make a simple tag shape from the smaller piece of white card, and apply the Pearlescent Orchid ink pad to the surface. Layer on to the larger piece of white card and trim to leave a small border. Stick the tag on to the front of the box with double-sided tape.

6 Place the crystal brad provided in to the centre of the paper flower and secure on to the flap of the box to finish.

WEDDING FAVOURS

There are many templates available to make gift boxes and bags in different shapes and sizes. This pretty confetti or favour box was made using Fiskars template 'Box 2' and K&Co 'Wedding' papers. *Stamps used: Magenta 'Retro Romance'.*

stamp smart

When using white embossing powder on white card the application of pearlescent ink on top will give the finished project a soft shimmer, which contrasts well with the white stamped image.

Vellum Dress

On this simple yet elegant card, the layers of stamped vellum are gently shaped by placing the pieces face down in the palm of the hand and rubbing with an embossing tool, which creates a realistic shape to the dress. Silicone adhesive holds the pieces in position. A border punch is used to create a lace effect from the paper and a silver ribbon adds an opulent touch.

1 Use the VersaMark™ ink pad to stamp the dress image on to one of the smaller pieces of white vellum.

2 Use the white embossing powder to heat emboss the image. Repeat with the other small piece of vellum so that you have two identical stamped and heat-embossed images.

3 Use the silver embossing powder to heat emboss a third image this time stamped on to the small piece of silver card. Cut all three images out, leave the silver image intact, cut the coat hanger from the first vellum image and cut the sash from the second vellum image.

4 Lay the pieces of stamped vellum face down in the palm of your hand and gently rub with the embossing tool in circular motions until the vellum begins to curl. Use silicone adhesive to stick the pieces together and leave to dry.

5 Fold the large piece of silver card in half to make the base card.

6 Use the silver ink pad to stamp the Florentine Scroll Background image on to the remaining piece of vellum. Use the Border punch to cut away the right-hand edge. Glue the vellum on to the front of the base card down the left-hand side only, as shown. Glue the ribbon on top to conceal the glued edge of the vellum.

7 Glue the layered dress on to the front of the base card. Glue the rose and beads on to the sash of the dress to finish.

YOU WILL NEED

Personal Impressions 'P1432P' stamp • Hero Arts® 'Florentine Scroll Background' stamp • VersaMark™ ink pad • Brilliance 'Platinum Planet' pigment ink pad • White embossing powder • Silver embossing powder • Two pieces of silver card, one 15 x 20cm (5⅞ x 7⅞in) for the base card, and one 12 x 5cm (4¾ x 2in) • Three pieces of white vellum, one 15 x 8cm (5⅞ x 3⅛in) and two 12 x 5cm (4¾ x 2in) • String of plastic pearl beads 6cm (2½in) in length • Fiskars Border punch • Silver ribbon 30cm (12in) in length • Satin rosebud • Embossing tool • Silicone adhesive • Glue stick

FINISHED SIZE 15 x 10cm (5⅞ x 4in)

Lotus Flower

This attractive layered flower makes a pretty alternative to a bow and can be placed on top of a shop-bought gift box. The flower is shaped in the same way as the dress pieces in the previous project. Place the pieces face up when shaping them so that the petals curl upwards and take care not to chip the embossing powder.

YOU WILL NEED

Funstamps '3D Flower 2' • VersaMark™ ink pad • Silver embossing powder • Two pieces of pale pink paper 7cm (2¾in) square • Deep pink paper 7cm (2¾in) square • Making Memories® crystal brad • Ready-made silver box • Pink ribbon 20cm (8in) in length • Embossing tool • Glue dot or 3D foam pad

FINISHED SIZE 6cm (2½in) square

1 Use the VersaMark™ ink pad to stamp the image on to one of the pieces of pale pink paper.

2 Use the silver embossing powder to heat emboss the image. Repeat on the other piece of pale pink paper and on the deep pink paper. Trim around the edges of all three images following the outline carefully.

3 Lay the pink stamped flowers face up in the palm of your hand and gently rub with the embossing tool until the petals begin to curl.

4 Layer the pieces together with the deep pink flower in the middle and secure with the brad in the centre.

5 Tie ribbon around the box lid and stick the flower on top using a glue dot or 3D foam pad.

stamp smart

To produce a fuller effect, stamp the image several times and use more layers. Patterned paper could also be used to make the flowers, however use fairly thin paper, as this will hold its shape better.

Japanese Journal

A simple knot is made from paper cord and complements the Oriental theme of this pretty concertina notebook. Fusible webbing is heated and covered with embossing powder to make a clever lace-effect background.

YOU WILL NEED

Aspects of Design 'Summer in the Orient' stamp sheet and clear acrylic mounting block • VersaMark™ ink pad • Gold embossing powder • Papermania 'Lilac Dragonfly' double-sided printed paper 14 x 12cm (5½ x 4¾in) • Cream paper 10.5 x 8.5cm (4⅛ x 3⅜in) • Narrow strips of lilac handmade paper 12cm (4¾in) long • The Stamp Man 'Concertina Card Kit' • Fan embellishment • Fusible webbing • Mizuhiki decorative paper cord 30cm (12in) in length • Lilac ribbon 20cm (8in) in length • General-purpose tacky craft glue • Glue stick

FINISHED SIZE 16 x 12cm (6¼ x 4¾in)

1 Assemble the concertina card as per the instructions. Glue the ribbon underneath the top and bottom covers prior to gluing on to the paper so that the ends are concealed.

2 Place the fusible webbing on top of the Lily Dragonfly scrapbook paper and use a heat gun to heat until holes start appearing. Sprinkle gold embossing powder on top, return the excess to the container and continue to heat. Stick on to the front cover with the glue stick.

3 Stick the strips of lilac paper to the top and bottom of the front cover. Using the VersaMark™ ink pad and gold embossing powder stamp and heat emboss the image on to the cream paper and glue on to the front cover.

4 Follow the manufacturer's instructions to make a knot from the decorative paper cord. Use the craft glue to stick the knot on to the fan, and the fan on to the bottom right-hand side of the stamped image.

stamp smart
Place acrylic mounting blocks on the corners of the fusible webbing prior to heating as this will help hold it in place until it begins to melt.

Psychedelic Purse

Iris folding is a paper folding technique involving laying strips across a shaped aperture. Depending on the papers used, an almost kaleidoscopic, psychedelic effect can be produced. This image is created by a special iris stamp, which includes the folding pattern.

1 Use the VersaMark™ ink pad to stamp the image on to the piece of pink card.

2 Use the gold embossing powder to heat emboss the image.

3 Cut the centre aperture from the stamped image. Turn the image face down and place the centre cut out face up within the aperture so that the folding pattern can be followed.

4 Cut the three sheets of printed paper into 4cm (1½in) strips and then fold each strip in half. Organize the strips into three piles of the same design.

5 Starting at number one on the pattern, place the first strip fold side inwards across the aperture and use double-sided tape to secure in place.

6 Take a piece from the second pile and stick at position 2 on the pattern using double-sided tape. Repeat with a strip from the third pile. Continue to follow the pattern in sequence. Take care not to tape the strips to the pattern as this is removed at the end.

7 Once the pattern is complete. Turn the card over and remove the centre template. Stick the image centrally on to the gold card using 3D foam pads.

8 Fold the aqua card in half to make the base card and stick the layered image centrally on to the front using double-sided tape to finish.

stamp smart
You can make your own iris folding paper by stamping patterns on to lightweight coloured paper then cutting it into strips.

YOU WILL NEED
Personal Impressions 'P1463S' stamp • VersaMark™ ink pad • Gold embossing powder • Three sheets of Dovecraft 'Retro Floral' 6 x 6in printed paper pack • Aqua card 12.5 x 25cm (5 x 10in) for the base card • Pink card 9.5cm (3¾in) square • Gold card 10.5cm (4⅛in) square • 3D foam pads • Double-sided tape

FINISHED SIZE 12.5cm (5in) square

Stamping School

This section looks at a few of the more advanced techniques that are worth mastering to perfect your 3D stamped creations. From choosing a colour scheme to applying paints and chalks, it's back to school to learn the secrets of stamping success.

Choosing colour

Colour is very important to the overall effect of a design. Choose colours that are strongly associated with the theme and style of the project. For example, use softer colours for feminine and baby projects, muted or aged colours for vintage projects, and primary colours for children's themes. To create a sense of harmony within the design, stick to shades of a similar colour, for example lilac, pink and blue. Using complementary colours (opposite to each other on the colour wheel, see right), for example red and green or purple and orange, will achieve a bolder statement. Sometimes just sticking to two or three well-chosen colours within a project will provide the most impact. When layering paper mounts or mats choose a paler mat behind an image that is mainly dark. If the main project is light, then choose a darker mat. When making multiple mats, alternate between layers of dark and light card. Using the same colours that appear in the image or photograph throughout the project will create a sense of unity.

Applying colour

Colouring techniques are used in the vast majority of stamping projects. Whether it is simply applying ink to a stamp, or painting the card after stamping, there are many different ways to add a splash of colour.

Inks

Aside from the basic practice of inking a stamp and using brush markers (**1**) (see How to stamp, pages 14–15), there are other ways that ink pads can be used to transfer colour to the paper.

Direct to paper is a technique where ink is applied straight on to the paper from the pad, using a gentle swirling motion to gradually build up colour (**2**). It is possible to blend several colours of ink together using this method.

Brayering is used to apply an even coat of ink to larger stamps. The brayer is rolled back and forth over the ink pad before rolling on to the surface of the stamp. A brayer is also used to apply dye ink on to glossy card, and this technique works well when using rainbow ink pads. The brayer is rolled over the ink pad and then applied directly to the surface of the paper. Stamping the card with a resist ink before brayering will produce an almost batik-style resist image.

stamp smart

Save your old ink pads rather than disposing of them, as they are ideal for using in the direct to paper technique, or for applying ink directly to the edges of torn paper for an aged effect.

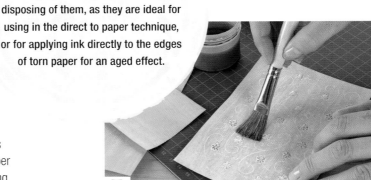

Paints

Watercolour paints are useful for creating light washes on paper (**3**), and for colouring in stamped images (**4**). Avoid using lightweight papers for painting on to, unless a fairly dry brush is used, as they may buckle or warp. Use smooth watercolour paper for stamping images that are going to be painted as the resulting stamped image will be crisp. Ensure that either dye or solvent inks are used for stamping, as these are less likely to smudge when the paint is applied.

Acrylic paints can be used in the same way as watercolours, they are suitable for use on most surfaces, and some have a sponge or felt dabber on the top of the bottle for easy application.

Dimensional paints usually come in bottles and the nozzle has an applicator tip. Droplets or beads are easily made by squeezing the bottle.

Pearlescent and metallic craft paints can be found ready mixed as pans or palettes, or as powders to add to other media. Some have interference effects and look different when painted on light coloured paper compared with darker paper. The powdered variety can be applied to images stamped with specialized inks such as VersaMark™, where the powder is gently brushed over the ink.

Pens and pencils

Leafing pens are similar to marker pens but produce a metallic coloured image such as copper, silver and gold. They are great for drawing metallic lines or colouring in.

Gel pens contain ink that has a gel appearance and are available in a wide range of shades and finishes, for example metallic, matte, neon and pastel. The pens can be used for colouring images or for writing with, and many work on a variety of surfaces.

Coloured pencils and pastels are great for colouring in stamped images (**1**). They are sold both individually and in sets and are easy to use. Shading and blending is achieved by simply varying the pressure on the tip. Watercolour pencils work in the same way as ordinary coloured pencils, but a paintbrush can be used to apply water over the top of the image to blend and soften the colours, creating a watercolour effect.

Chalks

Chalks are a subtle and pretty way to add colour to an image or to change the colour of the paper itself. Chalks can be blended together and hard lines removed using a cotton wool ball or sponge tipped applicator (**2**). Apply chalk to a torn paper edge for a pretty effect. Using a brown coloured chalk on creased paper will produce an aged or antique effect, as the chalk sits in the creases. Chalks can be used with resist inks, for example VersaMark™, where they will appear much darker when gently applied on top of the ink. Chalks usually come in palettes and lovely shimmer varieties are also available.

Glitter

Coloured glitter is available in different particle sizes. Children's glitter is larger in particle size, and very fine or ultra-fine glitter is the grown-up alternative. Firstly glue is applied with a fine-tip applicator; the glitter is sprinkled into the wet glue and allowed to dry. This type of glitter works well when colouring in images that have been stamped on to acetate and in particular mandala or medallion-style stamps (**3**). Glitter glue is also available and is usually applied directly from the tube or bottle; it is used for highlighting areas and has a subtler effect than traditional glitter.

Bleaching

Ordinary thin household bleach can be used to produce highlighted areas on coloured card. The image is first stamped and heat embossed on to coloured paper or card. Bleach is then applied using a paintbrush to lighten areas of the card. A heat gun will speed up drying time. Further applications will produce even lighter results. It is possible to lighten areas of coloured card with the bleach and then use coloured pencils to colour over the lightened areas. This will produce subtly coloured images set against strong backgrounds. Bleach is an irritant, so always wear gloves and ensure you do not get the product on your skin or in your eyes. Wear old clothes and protect all work surfaces by placing the card in an old box before spraying.

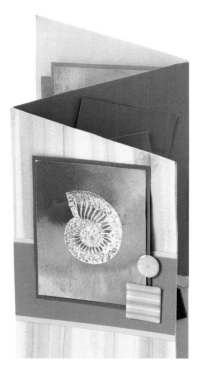

stamp smart

Use a mist bottle to spray bleach gently over card allowing the droplets to dry to reveal unique background papers. Great care must be taken when doing this.

Additional techniques

Finally, here are a few extra techniques to give your projects an individual finish and make them truly 'stamp out from the crowd'!

Tearing

Tearing paper rather than cutting it with a sharp edge can produce a lovely soft, textured finish. This effect can be exaggerated depending on the type of paper. The grain of the paper will determine how it will tear. Some papers will have a more pronounced grain than others, and some handmade papers do not have a definite grain. To test the grain, tear the paper both horizontally and then vertically – it will tear more easily and in a straighter line if torn along the grain.

A straight but natural edge can be obtained by laying a metal ruler on to the edge of the paper and tearing the paper against it (**1**). This method will give the most controlled torn edge. Torn paper can be crumpled and then coloured with diluted cold tea or distressing inks to produce an aged effect for use on heritage projects. Chalk, ink and metallic waxes can be rubbed along the torn edges of the paper to enhance the effect.

A chamfered edge is created by tearing paper towards you. The piece left behind has a white edge, which is simply the core of the paper (**2**). This can then be left alone for a nice contrast, or coloured. If a chamfered effect is not desired then tear the paper away from you, the result will be a torn natural edge with no white core showing.

A feathered edge is a different type of edge that works particularly well on thin fibrous handmade papers such as Mulberry paper. Use a small paintbrush to brush water along the edge of the paper then gently pull the edge away to give a soft feathered finish (**3**).

stamp smart

Using a bone folder to score the paper or card before tearing it will also give a neat, controlled tear.

Masking

Masking is used when stamped images overlap each other, or for creating images surrounded by a background image, as in many collage-style projects. The image is stamped on to a piece of scrap paper then cut away around the outline to create a mask. The main image is stamped on to the paper and then when dry, covered with the mask before stamping the background or overlapping image (**4**). When the mask is removed the completed image is revealed.

Dry embossing

Dry embossing involves using a brass stencil or template. Paper is taped face down on to the top of the stencil using low-tack masking tape. Both are then placed on top of a light box (or held against a window) so that the image can be seen through the paper. An embossing tool is used to gently rub over the stencil. Once the paper is removed from the stencil a raised 'embossed' surface is revealed in the shape of the template pattern. To help the embossing tool glide over the paper easily, rub the end of the embossing tool on to a candle (a tea light works well for this), alternatively rub the candle over the uppermost surface of the paper (the wrong side). On metal and foil surfaces, a dry-embossed effect can be achieved by drawing along the outline of the image with an embossing tool (**5**).

4

stamp smart

When creating a mask, cut out the image slightly smaller than the outline to prevent a halo effect occurring when the second image is stamped.

5

Templates

All templates on this page are 100%

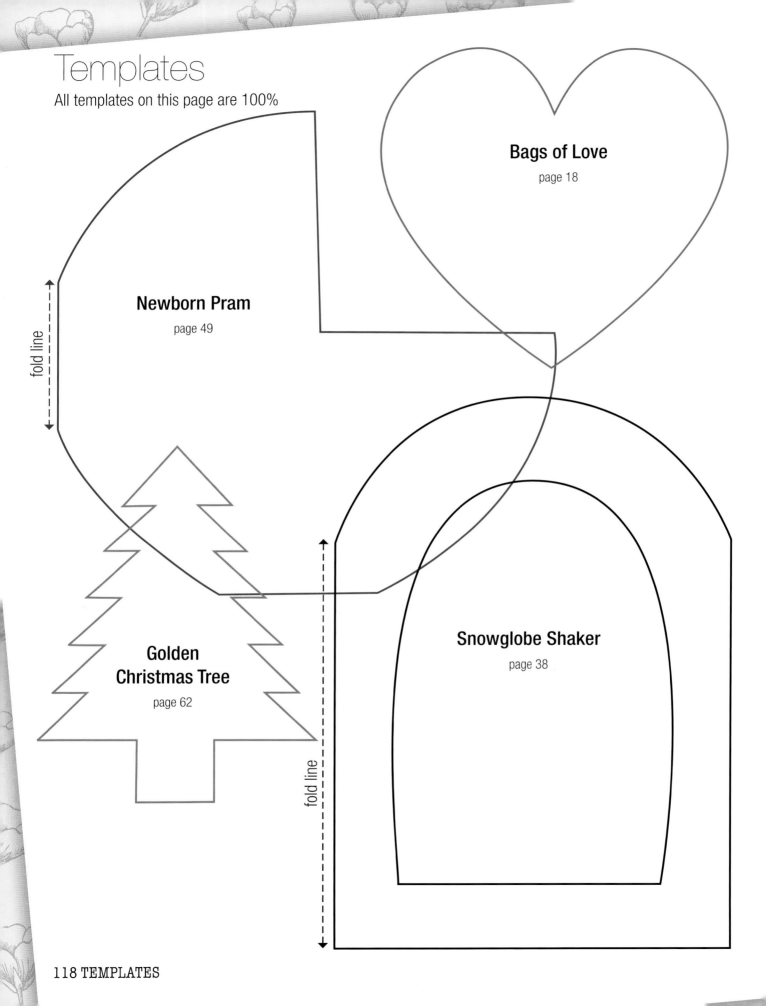

Bags of Love

page 18

Newborn Pram

page 49

fold line

**Golden
Christmas Tree**

page 62

Snowglobe Shaker

page 38

fold line

All templates on this page are 50%
(enlarge to 100% on a photocopier)

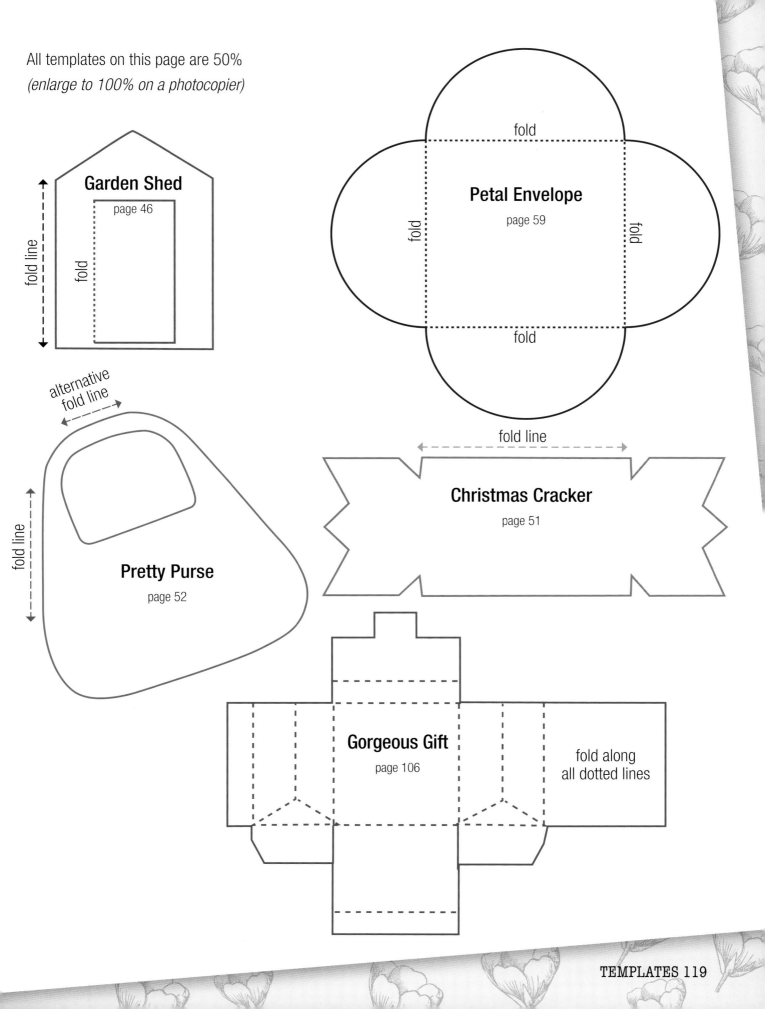

Garden Shed
page 46

fold line

fold

Petal Envelope
page 59

fold

fold

fold

fold

alternative
fold line

Pretty Purse
page 52

fold line

fold line

Christmas Cracker
page 51

Gorgeous Gift
page 106

fold along
all dotted lines

Suppliers

The You Will Need lists in the projects state the information you need to find the exact products used. These items were all available at the time of writing, however the author or publisher cannot be held responsible if manufacturers discontinue any of these items. If this should happen there are a wide range of similar products available which can be used to give equally good results. For further inspiration and handy hints visit my website, www.joannesanderson.com.

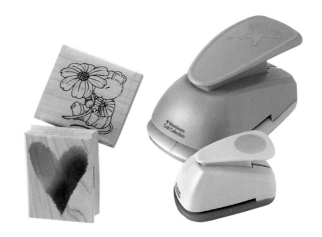

UK

All the items in the book were supplied by the following:

Crafts U Love www.craftsulove.co.uk
Hero Arts®, Doodlebug, ultra-fine glitter and glue
The Stamp Man www.thestampman.co.uk 01756 797048
Aspect of Design, acetate, Mizuhiki, Starburst Stains, fusible webbing, concertina books
MIC www.miccraft.net 01707 269999
Paper flowers and handmade papers
Southfields Stationers www.southfield-stationers.co.uk 0131 6544300
Card and paper
Elusive Images www.elusiveimages.com 01833 694914
Stamps
WhichCraft www.whichcraftuk.co.uk 01302 810608
Wide variety of stamps including Hero Arts®, Magenta and Woodware
The Scrapbook Shop www.scrapbookshop.co.uk 0191 3757515
Scrapbook papers
Rubbadubbadoo www.rubbadubbadoo.co.uk 01308 420802
Stamps
Horseshoe Crafts www.horseshoecrafts.co.uk 01691 690113
Stamping Sensations and Oyster Stamps
Crafty Individuals www.craftyindividuals.co.uk 01642 789955
Wide range of collage-style stamps

For details of local stockists contact:

Bramwells www.bramwellcrafts.co.uk
Hero Arts®, Inkadinkado Stamps, Paper Adventures
Trimcraft www.trimcraft.co.uk
DCWV, Dovecrafts
RichStamps www.richstamp.co.uk 01787 375241
Wide range of stamps including Personal Impressions
Impex www.impexcreativecrafts.co.uk 020 89000999
Embellishments
DoCrafts www.docrafts.co.uk
Papermania, See–Ds
Vesutor Ltd 01403 784028
Sandylion
Sizzix™ www.sizzix.com
Die cutting machine and dies
Katy Sue Designs www.katysuedesigns.com 01914 274571
Flower Soft™

USA

Art Institute Glitter www.artglitter.com 928-639-0805
Stamping equipment and embellishments
Clearsnap Inc www.clearsnap.com 360-293-6634
Inks, ink pads and stamps
Doodlebug Design Inc www.doodlebug.ws 801-966-9952
Papers and embellishments
EK Success www.eksuccess.com 800-524-1349
Paper, card, stamps and embellishments
Ellison www.ellison.com/corp 949-598-8822
Stamps and equipment
Hero Arts® Rubber Stamps Inc www.heroarts.com 510-652-6055
Stamps, stamping accessories and inks
Janlynn Corp (Stamps Happen Inc) www.janlynn.com 413-206-0002
Stamps
JudiKins Inc www.judikins.com 310-515-1115
Stamps and stamping accessories
McGill Inc www.mcgillinc.com 815-568-7244
Papercrafting materials
My Sentiments Exactly www.sentiments.com 719-260-6001
Stamps and stamping accessories
Penny Black Rubber Stamps Inc www.pennyblackinc.com 510-849-1883
Stamps, stamp sets and papers
Quickutz www.quickutz.com 801-764-2000
Stamping and papercrafting equipment
Ranger Industries www.rangerink.com 732-389-3535
Inks, stamps and papers
Stampendous Inc www.stampendous.com 714-688-0288
Stamps and stamping accessories
Stewart Superior Corp www.stewartsuperior.com
Inks and stamping equipment
Tsukineko Inc www.tsukineko.com 425-883-7733
Inks, including Memento™
Will'n Way www.willnway.com 800-325-4890
Clear stamps

Acknowledgments

Thank you to all my family and friends for their love and support, and to the suppliers for sending me all their wonderful products to use.

Index